Growing Up with Less Living with More

OrangeBooks Publication

1st Floor, Rajhans Arcade, Mall Road, Kohka, Bhilai, Chhattisgarh 490020
Website: **www.orangebooks.in**

First Edition, 2026

ISBN: 978-93-7426-297-9

Price: Rs. 329.00

Printed in India

Growing Up with Less

Living with More

Vinkal Kotangale

OrangeBooks Publication
www.orangebooks.in

Dedicated to my beloved Mother, whom I miss dearly, and to my Father and Sister, with deep gratitude for shaping who I am.

Why I Wrote This Book

For years, these stories lived quietly within me. I would often share these with my wife, the only person who truly knew all of these. From the small joys of hostel life to the silent kindness of strangers, she patiently listened as I recounted the moments that shaped me.

One day, she gently said, *"Why don't you write a book? Why not share these stories with the world and thank all those who helped you along the way?"*

That thought stayed with me. Not just the idea of writing, but the idea of offering gratitude. Gratitude to friends who stood by me. To strangers who helped without expecting anything. To the watchman who looked the other way so I could park my bicycle. To the teacher who waived a fee without a question. To the old man in the chilly winter mornings who simply showed up when I needed him.

This book is my thank you note to life, written through stories. Of acknowledging that while I may have grown up with less, I was never short of support, kindness, and quiet strength from those around me.

This is my way of honouring every friend, stranger, teacher, and loved one who, knowingly or unknowingly, helped me shape my journey.

Preface

Life in my early years was defined by less, less money, fewer choices, but somehow more joy. We didn't have much by today's standards, no fancy gadgets, no overflowing wardrobes, no endless choices. But what we had was enough. In fact, it was more than enough because it taught us how to make the most of what we had and how to value people, moments, and small acts of kindness. Scarcity didn't make life harder; it made it richer in ways I only understood much later.

Each chapter in this book is a story from those days, sometimes funny, sometimes moving, always honest. You will meet my childhood friends, my cousins, my hostel mates, my teachers, and strangers who became part of my journey. These moments shaped my values, my work, and the way I see the world today. These stories are about resilience, gratitude, and the unspoken bond between people who are "in the same boat."

As the years passed and I moved into a life of more comfort and convenience, I realised something important. While I now have more, the real wealth came from those years of less. Those days built the courage to take risks, to dream bigger, and to appreciate every small blessing.

Growing Up with Less Living with More is not just my story. In some way, it might be yours too. If you have ever felt the magic of a simple life or longed for the warmth of days when happiness didn't need much, I hope these stories take you back. And if you haven't, maybe they'll help you see that sometimes less truly gives us more.

It's not just a memoir. It's a love letter to a time when we had less, but lived more.

This book is my way of saying that a life lived with less can still be abundant, not in things, but in gratitude, courage, and connection. And if my stories make you smile, shed a tear, or bring you a moment of pause, then I will know that they have done their job.

Every story in this book is a piece of my real journey. The people, places, and events are all drawn from my life. Out of respect for the privacy of those who walked alongside me in these moments, I have chosen not to reveal their names.

Introduction

I grew up in a small town, in a simple nuclear family of four: my father, my mother, my elder sister, and me. With a small age gap between my sister and me, we were more like playmates than siblings, doing most things together. Both my parents were working, so for most of our childhood, our home was not just within our four walls, but it flowed into the warmth of our neighbours' homes.

After school, my sister and I would usually spend time at one of our neighbours' houses until my mother returned from work. Those evenings became a part of our daily rhythm. We would eat a snack there, sometimes join in their family conversations, and wait till we saw my mother's familiar figure walking back home. In those moments, our neighbours were like an extended family, filling the gaps when our parents were away.

For anyone who came to visit us, the direction was simple: *"Just look for the house with the papaya tree."* That tree, standing tall and visible even from the highway, became our landmark. Relatives, friends, or even someone delivering a letter all found their way to us by spotting it. Even today, when I close my eyes, I can see it swaying gently in the breeze, standing tall like a silent guardian of our childhood.

Our neighbourhood was made up of narrow lanes, small houses standing shoulder to shoulder, and people who knew each other like extended family. The grocery shop at the corner was more than a place to buy provisions, it was where neighbours exchanged news, children picked up toffees and sometimes borrowed items on credit when money was short. Everyone seemed to know everyone, and it was common for a neighbour to walk into our home without knocking, either to borrow sugar, share a piece of news, or simply sit and chat with my mother.

To us children, this world never felt small, but it was infinite. We played cricket in the open fields with our friends, defining our own rules. On some days, we would run to the nearby hill to fetch *sindhi*, a kind of local date-like fruit that grew there in plenty. Those playful climbs and the tangy-sweet taste of *sindhi* straight from the trees are still fresh in my memory.

Festivals were never about one household; they were for the whole lane. They belonged to everyone. During Diwali, we would all gather to burst crackers in the lane, and the entire street would glow with the light of *diyas*. On Holi, colours flew from one house to another until nobody could recognise who was who. Every year on Eid, our neighbour aunty would lovingly call us to her house to eat *sewai*, which we always waited for eagerly. Those celebrations stitched us together in ways that went beyond words.

Looking back, I realise that it was not just my parents and my sister who shaped my childhood, but also the neighbours, the shopkeepers, the playmates, and even the papaya tree outside our house. My small town gave me more than a place to live; it gave me a sense of belonging, security, and togetherness.

Whenever I think of my home, I don't just think of walls and roofs. I think of the sound of cricket in the fields, the amazing taste of *sindhi* fruits, the glow of Diwali lamps in every courtyard, and the warm taste of Eid *sewai* shared across families. That was my small town. That was my world.

And now, I invite you to step into that world, not only to know my journey, but perhaps to rediscover echoes of your own.

Contents

Section - III
Career Beginnings

Section - IV
Reflections and Life Lessons

Section - I

Childhood and Early Life

Where small joys and everyday struggles shaped resilience, gratitude and a heart full of stories.

1
The Clothes I Still Remember

I still vividly remember every piece of clothing I had during my childhood. Not because there were many, but because they were so few that each one was special, worn with pride, and deeply treasured.

New clothes were a rare treat for both my sister and me. They usually came once a year, mostly during Diwali. Sometimes, if we were lucky, we'd get something new during the summer holidays, a shirt or maybe a pair of sandals. There was no overflowing wardrobe, no confusion of "what to wear." Just a handful of well-worn clothes, and each had its own story.

One of my earliest and fondest memories is of a safari suit I had as a little boy. My mother used to call it my *Netajiwala suit*. It had golden embroidery and made me feel important, like a leader. I would proudly wear it along with a red coloured rose made of foam, gifted to me by one of our neighbourhood aunts. That flower stayed pinned to my shirt for days as a badge of joy, until it finally gave up.

But even when it wilted, the memory stayed fresh.

As I grew a bit older, I remember my cousin giving me a pair of blue jeans and sports shoes he had outgrown. He had used them well, and I wore them for years with pride. It wasn't about affordability. My parents could have managed a new pair easily. But back then, this was simply how things were done. If something still had life in it, it was passed on to someone younger, and we received it with the same joy as something new.

My sister, too, had her own small collection of cherished clothes. Each dress was special, worn on special occasions and remembered even today. Sometimes we would talk about our favourite clothes as if they were our friends. We never saw it as having less.

It was just the way we grew up, content and grateful.

In those days, we didn't dress for photos or for likes. We dressed for function, for tradition, and sometimes for celebration. Every piece of clothing was part of a memory, a festival, a school event, a visit to a relative's house, or a family wedding.

Today, when I look around and see closets filled with clothes, many barely worn, some forgotten with tags still on, I find it hard to even remember the last shirt I bought. Clothes have become too easy to get, too quick to replace. Somewhere along the way, they lost their meaning.

But those childhood clothes remain etched in my memory. That *Netajiwala suit,* the gifted jeans, my sister's favourite frock, they remind me of a time when simplicity didn't mean scarcity. They were not just garments; they were part of my growing-up years, where every garment was a gift, and each wear came with care.

Looking back, I realise that having fewer clothes made me value them more. Each item was a source of joy, not just utility. It taught me to take care of things, to wait patiently, and to be happy with what I had. In a world full of options today, I find comfort in those limited choices of the past.

Because in those simple clothes, I found a sense of identity, gratitude, and warmth that no expensive brand can replace.

Growing up like that taught me something precious, which I realise now that having less didn't mean enjoying less.

On the contrary, it meant cherishing more. More attention, more care, and more happiness in the little things.

> *"When you have only a few things, you don't just wear them. You remember them."*

Memory Note

That safari suit wasn't just clothing; it made me feel important. The foam rose, the embroidered fabric, my mother's words, all stitched a memory of pride, love, and joy in small things. I didn't know then that I was living a memory I'd return to so often, not for the value of the suit, but for how it made me feel seen, loved, and a little heroic.

2

The Shows I Never Watched and Still Loved

Growing up, our home had no cable television. It wasn't because we couldn't afford it, my parents simply had a rule of no cable television. There was a time when TV had only one or two channels, and cable TV, when it arrived, was seen as a privilege that not every home could afford. My parents believed it would distract us from our studies, so even though many of our neighbours had dozens of channels running all day, we stuck to that rule firmly.

Because of this, I never got to watch popular shows like *WWF* wrestling, cricket matches, or crime thrillers like *CID* and horror shows like *Aahat.*

My friends would talk excitedly about wrestlers like *Undertaker, Triple H, John Cena* and *Sable,* describing every move with passion.

I didn't know what these stars looked like or what the matches really felt like, but I listened closely and imagined it all.

One of the stories I remember best was about *Brian Lara's* incredible innings where he scored 400 runs in a Test match. My friends debated and admired that feat for days, and even though I hadn't seen it live on TV, hearing those stories made me feel connected to the excitement as I heard every detail from my friends. It was like being part of something larger, even from the sidelines.

That 400-run innings became legendary to me, a tale of brilliance and endurance that I admired even without seeing it happen.

Occasionally, I got lucky. Visiting my *Badepapa's* (Elder brother of my father) house meant I could catch a glimpse of *WWF*. Those moments felt special, almost like a celebration. Watching the action-packed matches was magical because it was so rare.

Sometimes, on other visits to another cousin's place, I would watch movies on CDs, and those simple pleasures became treasured memories. I still remember watching *Jumanji* starring *Robin Williams* and feeling the same thrill of adventure the kids experienced in that movie.

Looking back now, life has changed a lot.

Today, I can stream any movie or show at any time. But strangely, despite having such easy access, I rarely sit down to watch a full movie or spend hours binge-watching a series. Sometimes, I feel guilty spending that much time in front of a screen, like it's time taken away from more important things.

Back then, even the second-hand stories my friends shared about TV shows and cricket matches were enough to mesmerise me. I didn't need to see everything to feel the joy.

The wonder came from the sharing of stories, the excitement in their voices and the imagination that filled in the gaps.

I realise now that growing up without cable TV gave me a different kind of gift. It taught me patience, imagination, and the ability to enjoy simple pleasures. While others were absorbed by countless TV channels, I found happiness in the rare glimpses I would get and the stories shared by friends.

Those "less" moments felt larger than life.

My parents' strict rule may have felt limiting at times, especially when my friends talked about the latest shows I missed, but in hindsight, it was a quiet blessing. It shielded me from distractions and helped me focus on studies, friendships and other meaningful experiences. The absence of constant entertainment made me value every story I heard and every rare viewing opportunity.

That may be the reason I am able to recall all these moments so clearly and write them down in this book.

Life changes, priorities shift, and what we value evolves. But those early experiences taught me that you don't need much to find joy. Sometimes, the "less" we have is actually filled with more magic, more connection, and more meaning than the "more" we chase later.

I might have grown up without cable TV, without endless choices, but that "less" was rich with imagination, stories, and wonder.

And that's a treasure I still carry with me today.

> ***"Growing up with less didn't mean missing out, it meant living with more appreciation."***

Memory Note

Though I never watched those popular shows and matches myself, the stories my friends shared, like Brian Lara's legendary 400-run innings, filled my imagination and heart. My parents' no-cable rule helped me focus and made every rare viewing special, shaping how I value memories to this day.

3

The Brush I Never Had

As a child, I was always drawn to art. I loved sketching, shading, and playing with colours. I remember carefully replicating the image of *Chhatrapati Shivaji Maharaj* riding a horse and sketching the majestic *Buland Darwaza* from my history textbook. Those drawings weren't just lines on paper but were windows into a world I wanted to create.

Every summer, my cousin and I had a little tradition that we would pick a new class or hobby to explore together. One year, it was English grammar, another year, it was something else. But the year that stayed with me the longest was the one when we chose painting.

We were thrilled. We got our painting kits with a box filled with watercolours, a brush, and a small mixing palette. I still remember the comforting smell of new stationery and the pride while holding the brush as if I was about to create something magical.

But just before the classes were to begin, something unfortunate happened. I lost the small brush that came with my kit.

It might sound trivial to someone else, but for my father, it was more than a missing item. It was a sign of carelessness and not valuing what I had.

He said no.

No to the class. No to the fee. No to what felt like my first real chance to learn something I genuinely loved.

I tried to reason with him. I explained it was a small mistake and that I would be more careful. My cousin, seeing how badly I wanted to go, even tried speaking to him. But nothing worked.

Finally, I took a bold step for a child of my age. I approached the painting teacher and asked if he could visit my house and talk to my father. He agreed, perhaps he sensed how much this meant to me.

We rode back to my home on his bicycle. That cycle ride itself became memorable, not just for the nervousness I felt, but because something hilarious happened on the way. My cousin and I laughed about that for days, and even now, the memory makes me smile. But that story, I'll keep between us.

When we reached, the teacher stood in our modest living room and tried to convince my father that I had potential. That missing one brush shouldn't stop me from learning.

But my father didn't change his mind.

So that summer, my cousin went to painting class. And I went too, but not as a student. I'd quietly sit beside him, watching. I observed how he held the brush, how he chose colours, and how he blended water to create the right tone.

I couldn't paint, but I was learning all the same by just watching him.

I also observed the teacher experiment with Thermocol carving and learned by watching how he sharpened blades, how he used angles and scales to shape models. I still remember every detail, how he diagonally cut a shaving blade to get the perfect tip, and how he carved out a beautiful guitar from Thermocol.

One day, I tried it myself at home. I carefully recreated that guitar. It turned out quite well. I kept it for years as a reminder of not what I missed, but what I made possible despite it.

That summer taught me something deeper than technique; it taught me patience, observation, and resilience. I may not have had a brush, but I had a front-row seat to the beauty of creating something from nothing.

Years passed. Life moved on. A busy work life. Painting remained in a quiet corner of my heart unforgotten and untouched.

Then, during my MBA internship, I found myself with free time in the evenings. One day, I came across a local art class.

On impulse, I enrolled.

I remember opening that bottle of linseed oil and dipping a brush into colour after so many years. The scent, the texture, the moment, all came rushing back like an old friend. My hands moved with surprising ease, guided by memories etched from that silent summer long ago. It felt like reuniting with an old friend.

Since then, painting has become a part of who I am. I have created many artworks, some abstract, some inspired by nature and some just pure emotion on canvas.

And the person who now supports it the most?

My father.

He cheers for every painting I make. The same man who once said no now encourages every stroke.

But the story doesn't end there.

Today, he is the one who drops my daughter to her painting class. And to her music class. And to her dance class. He waits there till she finishes, sometimes reading the newspaper, sometimes chatting with other parents. Quietly and patiently.

I often watch them from a distance, my daughter walking into a world I once only watched from the sidelines, and my father standing behind her like a silent pillar.

Maybe he is giving her what I couldn't have.

Or maybe this is his way of saying, *"I see you now. I am proud of you."*

> ***"Life comes full circle in the most unexpected ways. And sometimes, the brush you never had leads you to paint stories that stay forever."***

Memory Note

What I couldn't learn with a brush, I learned by watching. I also learned that not having something does not stop learning; it only changes the way we learn. Today, my biggest supporter is the same father who once said no. Sometimes, love waits to find the right canvas.

4

A House That Made Me Stronger

When I was in seventh standard, a change became necessary. There was no English-medium school in my hometown beyond sixth standard, and my parents knew that, for me to have a chance at better opportunities, I needed to switch. So, it was decided that I would move to the district town and enrol in a convent school.

But such changes, though logical on paper, are never simple in reality. My mother was a working woman, and government job transfers take time. My father couldn't leave either. The solution? I would temporarily stay at my maternal aunt's house, whom I fondly called *Mothiaai* (Mother's Elder Sister) until the family could relocate.

It was the first time I would live away from home.

Until then, my world was simple and familiar, waking up to my parents' voices, the smell of my mother's tea, and the comfort of my own bed. Shifting to a new house, even if it belonged to a close relative, felt like stepping into a different world. My *Mothiai's* home was quiet, more structured, and ran on a rhythm different from ours. I had to adapt quickly.

At first, I felt a strange mix of discomfort and determination. I missed home, but I also knew that this phase mattered. I was here for a purpose: to learn and to grow.

Slowly, I began to change. I started doing things for myself, without waiting for someone to remind or guide me. I became more self-reliant. *Mothiaai* expected me to be responsible, not in a harsh way, but with gentle firmness. That trust made me rise to the occasion.

My uncle, a calm and thoughtful man, had a habit of reading the newspaper religiously every morning. Observing him, I picked up the habit myself. Initially, I just flipped through the pages.

But soon, I found myself reading headlines, then editorials, and slowly developing curiosity about the world beyond school textbooks. One memory that stands out is when I wrote a letter to the editor in *Lokmat,* a Marathi newspaper, about farmer suicides. I remember carefully drafting it and dropping it into the red post-box at the bus-stand, filled with nervous excitement.

To my surprise, it was published. That moment lit a quiet spark, and I realised my voice could matter.

Since then, reading *Lokmat* has become a daily habit and has stayed with me for life. It helped me in exams, in interviews, and, more importantly, in becoming an aware individual.

Academics were taken seriously in *Mothiaai's* house. My cousin brother and one sister were older than me, while another sister was younger; all of them were focused students. We each had our designated seats and would study together often for hours in complete silence.

That quiet discipline had a profound impact on me.

It taught me patience, focus, and how to approach studies systematically by breaking down chapters, planning ahead, and staying with it even when it got tough.

But it wasn't just academics that shaped me there; it was also the emotional environment.

What touched me deeply was how *Mothiaai* never made me feel like a guest. I was never treated as an "extra mouth to feed" or a burden. I was included in every family discussion, every small celebration, every Sunday ritual. My cousins didn't see me as an outsider either. They helped me with my studies and even protected me like a younger brother when needed.

Mothiaa's house didn't just give me shelter, it gave me a sense of belonging.

Those years also made me grateful to my school teachers, who helped me adjust to a new environment. Their discipline and encouragement gave me the confidence I needed to stand on my own. At a stage when everything felt new and a little intimidating, their patient guidance made the classroom feel less like a challenge and more like a place of possibilities.

Around the same time, another person quietly shaped my journey. My tuition teacher!

I had joined a home tuition class nearby where a ma'am used to teach me with incredible patience. That little room, simple as it was, became the breeding ground where my foundation was built strong. All my doubts, no matter how small, were welcomed and addressed with clarity and ease. For a student trying to adjust to a new school, new syllabus, and new surroundings, her guidance was priceless. Looking back, I realise she not only strengthened my academics but also gave me the confidence to ask questions and to never feel shy about learning. Even today, when I solve problems with a calm, systematic approach, I silently remember those mornings in her class and the way she believed in me.

Over time, this arrangement of me staying at *Mothiaai's* house became more than temporary. Even after my parents moved to a nearby place on transfer, I continued to stay with my aunt during exam season, especially for tuition classes and test series. It was understood that her home was the best environment for focused study. And each time, she welcomed me back as if I had never left.

Looking back, I realise how critical that phase was.

It was in that house that I learned to be responsible without being told.

It was in that house that I learned the value of time, the joy of discipline, and the power of quiet encouragement.

It's easy to look at such times as simply "adjustments" or "compromises," but I now see them as gifts. Without that phase, I wouldn't have grown into who I am.

Many years have passed now. But whenever I sit to reflect on what truly shaped me, my mind quietly walks back to that seventh standard boy, nervously stepping into a new house with a schoolbag and a head full of doubts.

And then I think of my *Mothiaai,* who opened her door and her heart without hesitation. I think of my uncle, whose quiet habits inspired mine. I think of my cousins, who made space for me in their world.

That house didn't just make me stronger, it made me better.

I hope *Mothiaai* knows what a difference she made. Maybe I never said it aloud then. Maybe I still find it difficult to say even now. Her soft, steady, and encouraging support meant the world to me.

> ***"She didn't just host a child. She shaped a life, and for that, I'll be forever grateful."***

Memory Note

That year away from home changed me in quiet ways I only understood much later. Living in my aunt's house taught me how to manage myself, value time, and stay steady even when things felt unfamiliar. I did not realise it then, but those simple days were shaping my confidence and my habits for life. My aunt did more than give me a place to stay; she gave me the space to grow.

5

Where the Journey Began

For many city dwellers, the ST (State Transport) bus may feel like a topic "out of syllabus," a system they rarely think about, maybe even find outdated or unnecessary. But for people like me, and many others from small towns and villages, the ST bus was not just a way to travel. It was the only way to travel.

More than that, it became a part of our lives, a constant, a routine, a companion in our growing-up years, and it became a means of realising our dreams. In my own journey so far, ST has played a crucial role. For me, the ST bus was much more than just a mode of transport.

It was a lifeline. It connected me to my school, to my education, to my dreams. It carried not just students like me, but also the weight of our hopes, struggles, and ambitions.

When I was in the 9th standard, my mother got transferred to a nearby village. As a result, we had to move there from the city. Life changed overnight. I was still studying in my district-town school, so we had to find a way to continue that.

And the only option was, yes, you guessed it right. The ST bus!

Every morning, I had to catch the 8:15 AM ST bus for a 30 to 40-minute ride winding through a few sleepy villages until we reached the district ST stand. From there, my day would unfold: tuition classes, test series and then school.

My schedule was packed, but I didn't mind.

I had goals, and I was ready to work for achieving those.

In the evening, I relied on the 5:10 PM ST bus to take me back home.

I still remember how I had to get special permission from our Principal sir to leave the last period 15 minutes early, just so I wouldn't miss that evening bus. His support was one of the many small kindnesses that made a big difference in my life. Sometimes, it's the small gestures from people around us that make a huge impact in our lives. I will always be grateful to him for that support.

Everything in my life, my studies, school, and coaching all revolved around two bus timings. My entire day was built around that schedule. And I followed that routine with complete dedication. Not once did I complain. Not once did I feel it was a burden.

I just accepted it as a part of life.

And how can I forget the monthly pass? Every month, I stood in the long queue at the district bus stand to get my travel pass renewed. The line often seemed never-ending, full of school and college students like me. But we all waited patiently, knowing how important that small piece of paper was. Without the pass, affording daily travel would have been tough.

That queue was another part of our routine and a shared experience that built patience and discipline.

There was a time when catching the ST bus meant planning, being on time, and adjusting my day around its schedule. Now, with everything just a click away, I rarely feel the need to follow a routine. Somewhere along the way, comfort has replaced commitment.

A classic example of how convenience can quietly breed complacency.

Travelling daily on the crowded, sometimes unpredictable ST buses taught me practical wisdom. It showed me the beauty of patience and perseverance.

It introduced me to the diverse lives of fellow passengers who were all moving forward with their own hopes and struggles.

Today, life looks very different. I sit in air-conditioned cars, travel across cities and countries, and often find it hard to stick to a fixed timetable.

Perhaps it's because I now have the freedom of flexibility.

But somewhere, I know that this convenience has quietly made me a little less disciplined.

Back then, I had no choice. I had to be ready before 8:15 AM, or I'd miss the bus. I had to leave school early, or I'd miss the evening bus. There were no second chances, no Plan B.

That pressure taught me something that comfort never could: the importance of showing up on time, every time!

Travelling daily on a crowded bus, I would come across all kinds of passengers. I met farmers, traders, students, working women, and elderly villagers, each carrying their own story. I saw how hard people worked. I saw how some people travelled long distances every day just to earn a little money.

Those rides opened my eyes to the real world and taught me humility, empathy, and above all, resilience. Even when things were not easy, people kept going. And I learned to do the same.

Today, as I travel internationally and navigate busy airports, I never feel overwhelmed or anxious. I credit that calmness to the years spent travelling by ST, and life lessons learned standing on *Platform 13* of the district ST stand that have stayed with me for life.

Although my life no longer depends on the ST bus, I deeply believe that it remains as essential today as it was twenty years ago, especially for rural areas. For countless students, small traders, farmers, and milk vendors, ST buses are still the backbone of daily life.

The ST bus is more than just transportation. It's a symbol of growing up with less, with limited resources and simple means, yet living with more: more resilience, more gratitude, more life lessons.

Even now, when I see an ST bus on the road, something stirs in me. It reminds me of where it all started. Of how far I have come. And of the thousands of students like me, still boarding that early morning bus with quiet hopes in their eyes.

I truly hope that the ST service continues for generations to come. It may not make headlines or win awards, but it quietly carries the dreams of so many, and that, in itself, is priceless.

> ***"Some journeys may end, but the lessons they leave behind continue for a lifetime."***

Memory Note

In those days, I didn't have a choice. ST was the only way. But looking back, I realise it gave me far more than just a ride to school. It gave me discipline, patience, and the quiet strength to carry on. The sound of the bus horn, the rush to grab a window seat, the conductors who recognised regulars and the monthly pass. Each detail lives in my memory, rich and intact. Today, I may not travel by ST anymore, but every time I pass one, I see a part of my childhood moving forward. Strong, steady, and still serving.

6
The BSNL Guards and the Cycle of Gratitude

As I have shared before, my daily routine involved taking the bus from my village to the district town for school and tuition. But my journey didn't end when the bus stopped; it had another leg too. Once I got off at the bus stand in town, I still had to travel across the city for tuition and other classes. For that, I had my trusted bicycle.

That cycle was my lifeline in the town. Without it, I would have spent a lot of time walking long distances and got tired even before my classes began. But there was one problem, where to keep it safe while I was away.

This is where my father stepped in. With his humble network, he arranged for me to park the cycle inside a BSNL (Bharat Sanchar Nigam Limited) office, which was conveniently located right near the bus stand. It was a simple arrangement, but to me, it was a big relief.

For a few days, everything went smoothly. I would get off the bus, walk into the BSNL compound where my cycle was parked, take it, and then ride off to school and classes. In the evening, I'd return the same way to park my cycle and board the bus back home.

Then one evening, as I entered, the two guards at the gate stopped me. *"Tumhe yahan cycle rakhaneki ki permission kisne di?"* (Who gave you the permission to park here?) one of them asked in a stern tone.

I froze, unsure what to say. My heart was racing. I mumbled, *"Sirf aaj ke liye… main ise kal hata doonga"* (Just for today… I'll remove it tomorrow). They let me go, but I walked away feeling nervous.

The very next day, something changed. My father must have quietly spoken to someone inside, maybe an officer he knew or a friend who knew the guards. I never asked for the details. But from that day on, neither of the guards stopped me again. Still, I always walked in quietly, parked my cycle quickly, and left without making eye contact.

Even today, after all these years, I sometimes dream about being stopped at that gate.

Now, when I look back, I realise what a big difference that small act of kindness made. Without that parking spot, I might have missed tuition classes, lost time, or even struggled to keep up in studies. And those classes were important. They shaped my learning and gave me the confidence to aim higher.

The BSNL guards might never have realised it, but by letting me park that cycle, they indirectly gave me more time, more safety, and more peace of mind to focus on my studies. Sometimes, the opportunities we get are not grand scholarships or expensive coaching but the tiny allowances and small openings that help us keep going.

In my 10th board exams, I scored really well, just a little short of making it to the state merit list. I felt proud and also thankful. One of the first things I wanted to do was to visit the BSNL office, not with my cycle this time, but with a box of sweets.

So, I went back to the office, and I found the same guards at the gate. They looked at me in surprise, wondering why I was there. When I told the guards my results and said, *"Mein apko thank you bolne aya hu"* (I came to thank you), they looked at me with surprise and pride. Maybe they had silently followed my progress, or maybe it was just the joy of seeing a young boy remember them. Either way, their faces lit up. The expression on their faces is something I still remember.

We exchanged only a few words that day, but the moment has stayed with me far longer than any formal congratulation or certificate. Gratitude has a way of making small events shine brighter in memory.

That day taught me something valuable that not all help is big or obvious. Sometimes it's a quiet gesture, a simple allowance, that ends up changing someone's path.

Even today, when I pass by a BSNL office or see a security guard on duty, I am reminded of them, their quiet cooperation, their silent nod that allowed me to keep moving forward. In the grand scheme of my life, it might seem like a tiny thing. But for a boy with little to spare except determination, it was huge.

Wherever they are today, I hope they know that their simple act is a part of my story of who I became. I hope they realise that sometimes, giving someone a little space can literally help them go a very long way.

> ***"Sometimes, the smallest permissions open the biggest doors."***

Memory Note

I never learned their names, and they may never know the role they played in my journey. But their quiet kindness had made my path easier, and I never forgot it. Even today, I feel a deep gratitude for those silent supporters whose small acts carried such great weight in my journey. Some journeys move forward because someone, somewhere, chose not to stop us.

7
The Fire at the Bus Stop

When I was in my final year of school, winter mornings in my village felt colder than ever. I used to travel every day to the district town for school and tuition. The bus ride itself was cold, but the real challenge came when I reached the town and waited for my tuition classes to begin.

That year, my tuition had started an early morning mock test series for our board exam preparation. This meant I had to catch the first bus. The early hours were freezing, and the wind would cut through my sweater.

By the time I sat down to write the test, my hands would be so numb that my handwriting looked messy and my fingers felt stiff for the first 30 minutes. It was frustrating because I had studied well, but I couldn't write the way I wanted.

In those days, small - town bus stands didn't have waiting rooms or much shelter. People, especially daily travellers, often lit small fires on the roadside in winter using dry sticks, cardboard, or paper to fight off the cold, something the younger generation may find hard to imagine today.

One morning, as I got off the bus, I noticed an old man sitting near the bus stand. He had lit a small fire using dry sticks, pieces of cardboard, and scrap paper. He sat there quietly, rubbing his hands to keep warm.

The next day, I went a little closer to the fire. The warmth felt like instant relief after the biting cold. The old man looked at me and gave a gentle smile.

I smiled back.

The day after, when I came again, he shifted slightly to make space for me to stand near the fire.

Soon, it became part of my daily routine. Before heading to my tuition, I would spend a few minutes by that fire, letting my hands warm. That little warmth made a big difference.

I could write faster and more neatly in the tests, and my mornings didn't feel as harsh.

The old man didn't know how much he was helping me. We never exchanged names or spoke more than a smile, but in those moments, there was a quiet kindness.

Looking back now, I realise that what he gave me was far more than heat. That fire wasn't just a physical comfort but a reminder that in the middle of our struggles, kindness can appear in the simplest forms. He didn't ask for anything in return, didn't even seem to think of it as an act of generosity. For him, it was just a way to get through the cold mornings. For me, it was the difference between starting the day in pain and starting it with a small bit of hope.

That fire at the bus stop, and the old man who tended it, taught me about humanity without saying a single word. Even today, I remember his face and those warm flames.

Life has changed since then. I have more comfort now. But I carry that lesson with me to quietly help others when I can, without expecting anything in return.

Because "Growing Up with Less Living with More" is not just about money or comfort. It's about valuing the moments, the people, and the kindness that helped us along the way. It's about remembering the old man at the bus stop and making sure that, in someone else's story, we are the fire.

> ***"A small flame can light a lifetime of gratitude."***

Memory Note

A small fire on a cold winter morning, shared by a stranger, gave me more than warmth. It gave me strength, comfort, and a quiet lesson in kindness. That moment taught me that even the simplest acts can change someone's day, and sometimes, their life.

8

The Lamp That Lit My Dreams!

When I stepped into the 11th standard, life took a sudden turn. My school and tuition timings were no longer aligned with the bus schedule from my hometown. The logistics simply didn't work anymore. So, after much thought, my family and I decided that I would shift to the district town where my school was located for those two crucial years. That way, I could stay closer to my school and tuition classes, and not lose precious hours each day just commuting.

I moved into a small rented room with my cousin, also a student. It was a modest arrangement. Just two young boys trying to manage food, money, studies, and the silence of living alone away from family for the first time. We were on our own. And even though we didn't talk about it much, both of us felt the weight of responsibility in our own ways.

Those were the days when "load shedding" was a term everyone knew well, planned power cuts by the electricity board, especially during evenings. Often, the electricity would go out just when I sat down to study.

For today's generation, it might be hard to imagine, but back then, an emergency rechargeable light itself was a big luxury. It was costly, and not every household could afford one, so during long power cuts, many of us simply had to adjust in the dark.

Sensing this, my mother had lovingly bought me a rechargeable emergency lamp. It was a small white lamp with a handle and a purple body cover, one of those common ones found in many homes back then. I knew it wasn't cheap for us. It was a small act, but I knew it wasn't easy for her.

That light worked well for some time and became my companion, but one evening, it just gave up. I took it to a local repair shop, hoping for a quick fix, and the person there tried to fix it. The shopkeeper tried something with the wires and battery. But instead of repairing it, he made it completely useless. It wouldn't even flicker anymore.

I was scared, not of the dark, but of upsetting my mother. I didn't want to ask her for a new one. I knew things were tight at home, so I quietly let it go.

That's when I turned to a friend who ran a hardware shop. I bought a simple kerosene lantern from him, the kind with a glass chimney and a small wick that needed trimming.

It cost me only 30 Rupees. It was humble. It had no buttons, no batteries, just a soft flame behind glass. That lamp became my silent companion.

It didn't flicker like my old torch or die out like the power did. It didn't buzz like a tube light or make that sharp LED brightness. It glowed gently, like it respected the silence of the room. And in that glow, I studied sometimes until midnight, sometimes fighting sleep, but always focused. Slowly, I got used to it. In fact, I started liking it.

It trained my mind to concentrate despite limitations. The dim, steady glow taught me patience, rhythm, and deep focus, something today's well-lit, distraction-filled rooms often fail to do. That lamp taught me something more deeper, it showed me how to keep going when things stop working. How to find alternatives. How to not complain and most importantly, how to stay steady, even in dim light.

Even when I moved on, completed engineering, got a job, and shifted to better homes, I carried that kerosene lamp with me. It became a souvenir, a quiet reminder of those tough but formative days.

It was about remembering the boy who chose not to complain, who chose to adjust, and who learned that light doesn't always come from electricity; sometimes, it comes from within.

Today, when I look at it, I don't just see an old lamp. I see a younger version of myself, someone who was scared but also someone who was determined too. Someone who didn't complain. Someone who found light in unlikely places.

> ***"That lamp didn't just light up my room.***
> ***It lit up my journey."***

Memory Note

That old lamp now sits on a corner shelf in my home not as a backup source of light, but as a reminder. Of a phase in life when things were limited but values were rich. Of how, sometimes, a small flame can light up a very long path.

9

The Maths Class That Multiplied Kindness

After passing out from the 10th standard, I took admission in the most sought-after junior college in our town. It was a government college, known for its merit-based admissions and high academic standards. Students from across the district, urban, rural, and tribal, aspired to get in. It was like a *sangam*, a confluence, where students from different backgrounds, different schools, and different boards came together.

If I may give you an analogy, it felt like the *Mumbai* of junior colleges. A true cosmopolitan mix in the academic sense.

Initially, everyone stuck to their previous school groups. There was an air of hesitation, as students tried to find comfort in familiarity while figuring out their place in this new environment.

But unexpectedly, I was chosen as the Class Representative (CR) within the first semester. It wasn't something I had aimed for, but once the responsibility came, it pushed me out of my comfort zone.

It turned out to be a blessing in disguise.

My role as a CR required me to interact with almost everyone in the class. Through this, I gradually began to form bonds with students from all walks of life.

One such bond became very special. That's when I met a classmate from a remote, Naxalite-affected region of our district. He stayed in a government-run hostel nearby, along with another friend who came from a similar background. He was soft-spoken, sincere, and came from a humble farming family.

Despite all the odds, he had made it into this prestigious college, which is an achievement in itself. Over time, we became good friends.

One day, he quietly told me that he was struggling with Mathematics.

He had been trying hard, but without proper guidance, he was falling behind. He said he wanted to join the same Maths tuition class I attended, but couldn't afford the fees. I could see the hesitation and disappointment in his eyes as he spoke. It wasn't easy for him to admit this.

I was at a loss. I truly wanted to help him, but the coaching class fee wasn't a small amount. I couldn't just ask my parents to sponsor him. We weren't exactly well-off ourselves. It bothered me deeply. Here was a bright student with dreams, only being held back because of financial constraints.

Now, let me give you some context here. Like most students preparing for their board exams, I was heavily dependent on coaching classes, especially for subjects like Maths. While not as expensive as they are today, even back then, the fee for coaching classes was a significant burden for many families. My parents managed to pay for my classes, but I couldn't ask them to sponsor someone else, no matter how much I wanted to help.

I felt truly helpless at first. But then some random thought gave me a bit of hope. I shared a strong rapport with my Maths tuition teacher. I had been his student since the 10th standard and had topped his institute that year. He knew me not just as a student, but as someone sincere and trustworthy. He appreciated me for my sincerity and punctuality, and I had always felt comfortable speaking with him.

That bond gave me the courage to approach him with a request that, even in that moment, felt a little bold.

After a bit of hesitation, I decided to take a chance. Gathering all my courage, I approached him after class the next day and said, *"Sir, I have a friend who really needs help in Maths. He's very sincere but can't afford the tuition fee. Can you allow him to attend the classes without charging him?"*

What happened next is something I will never forget.

Sir looked at me, smiled slightly, and simply said, *"Ask him to attend all the classes regularly."*

That's it. He didn't ask me who the student was. He didn't want to know his background, his grades, or how long he planned to attend. There were no conditions. Just trust.

It was such a small sentence, but it meant so much.

In that moment, I felt a wave of gratitude wash over me. Not just because my friend was getting the help he needed, but because of the implicit trust my teacher placed in me. He didn't need proof, explanation, or justification. He just believed me.

He trusted my word, perhaps because of the faith I had earned as a student, but also because he believed in helping quietly and generously. That quiet gesture of belief meant the world to me.

My friend joined the classes from the very next day. He was regular, attentive, and worked very hard. Over time, he improved tremendously. He went on to do really well in his board exams. Later, he pursued engineering and eventually became a successful Chemical Engineer, completing his degree from a well-known college.

That one decision by a teacher who could have easily said no changed a life. And perhaps, in a small way, changed mine too.

Years have passed since then, but the memory of that time remains vivid in my heart. What stayed with me wasn't just the act of kindness itself, but the way it was offered. Silently, without expectation and without judgment.

My teacher didn't offer a free class. He offered dignity, respect, and belief.

Looking back, I realise we didn't have many resources growing up. We didn't have access to expensive coaching classes, brand-name schools, or financial security. We didn't even have that much confidence in ourselves at times. But what we did have was an ecosystem of good people like teachers who believed in us, friends who helped each other, and families who supported us in every way they could.

That one instance in the Maths class may seem small from the outside, but for my friend and me , it changed the course of our lives. It reminded me that sometimes, all it takes is one person's trust to spark a lifetime of possibilities.

That Maths class didn't just teach formulas or problem-solving. It taught something much deeper. It showed me how far trust and compassion can go.

Today, whenever I see young students trying to make it through challenges, I remember those days and silently hope they, too, find someone who helps quietly, who trusts unconditionally, and who multiplies not just knowledge, but kindness, just like how my teacher believed in me.

Perhaps that's why, in almost every corporate role I have held so far, I have chosen to volunteer with the Learning & Development teams, training juniors and sharing whatever I can. I also mentor students stepping into professional courses, hoping to be that small helping hand I once received.

In many ways, the kindness shown to me in that Maths class continues to ripple forward, multiplying still.

> ***"Growing up with less didn't stop us. In fact, it gave us more, more empathy, more courage, and more gratitude."***

Memory Note

Sometimes, the smallest acts of belief can create the biggest impact. It wasn't just a Maths class. It was a quiet moment of belief. A teacher trusting my word, a friend getting a chance, and kindness multiplying without a sound. Sometimes, it's not resources that shape futures, but people who choose to believe without asking why.

Section - II

Hostel and College Days

Years of scarcity, friendship, and resourcefulness

where jugaad and camaraderie

became survival skills.

10

The Journey That Shaped My Journey

I always wanted to become a doctor. It wasn't just a childhood dream; it was how I imagined my future. But I missed the government medical college cut-off by a few marks. Everyone around me expected me to repeat the entrance exam the next year. But instead of going down that road, I made a strange decision: I switched paths and applied for Engineering.

It was a surprising choice, even to me. Maybe I lacked the confidence, or maybe I just didn't want to sit through another year of uncertainty.

Interestingly, it was a doctor practising in my village who made me rethink medicine. He never said it outright, but his quiet frustration and occasional comments like, *"If I had a second chance, I'd choose something else,"* stuck with me. When I had to decide whether to repeat the medical exam or switch paths, his words quietly influenced me. Maybe he didn't intend to, but somehow, he did.

However, fortunately, I got into one of the top Engineering colleges in Mumbai. The seat allotment notice came online with just three days to report. My father, calm and resourceful as ever, managed to get us a reservation on the least preferred option: *The LTT Express.*

I still remember that journey. I don't think I'll ever forget it.

The train departed around 11 in the morning. About an hour in, it came to a halt at some unknown station and didn't move for the next six hours.

Six hours!

Outside my window, I watched life go on. A woman squatted by the tracks, started a small fire, cooked some roti and sabzi, fed her child, and then even managed to take a nap. Meanwhile, we were still waiting, baking in the heat, anxious and exhausted.

We reached *Kurla* Station the next day, around the same time, completing a 24-hour ordeal that felt like it stretched a lifetime. From there, we took an auto to the college campus in *Andheri.*

The moment I stepped inside the campus, I felt completely out of place. The students around me were well-dressed, polished, and confident. I was scared and low on confidence, feeling like an outsider in a new, intimidating world.

Amid the admission process, I was asked to make a DD from a nearby Bank. While filling out the form, I asked a simple question to a man in crisp white clothes. Instantly, a gunman standing nearby immediately gave me a stern look as if to say, *"How dare you?"* But the man just smiled gently, signalling him to relax, and answered me politely. I later saw the government vehicles parked outside and realised he was a senior government officer who had come along with his son for admission.

That brief interaction, his humility and decency have left a lasting impression on me.

Years later, when I too became a government officer, I often found myself thinking about that afternoon. His calm dignity, his willingness to treat a nervous young stranger with respect, shaped the kind of officer I wanted to be, not just efficient, but also approachable. It reminded me that sometimes, the way we treat people in passing can stay with them for a lifetime.

That afternoon, I had lunch at a roadside stall near the college, four rotis and some sabzi for just ₹20. Funny thing is, I never ate there again in all four years of my engineering. I am not sure why I chose that stall that day, but I am glad I did. It's a memory I carry with me more vividly than most fancy meals.

After the admission formalities, someone told us that catching the return train from *Dadar* would be easier. We didn't have a reserved ticket, but we took our chances and boarded the *LTT Express* again, this time in a reserved coach with just general tickets. As expected, the TTE caught us. I nervously tried to explain the situation that I was new to Mumbai, had just taken admission, and didn't know the proper rules. He looked at me for a long moment, then smiled and said, *"My son studies in the same college."* Instead of penalising us, he asked us to shift to the general compartment.

That night, I sat on the floor of the general coach all the way home. The coach was overcrowded, the air thick with the smell of sweat, food, and iron. And yet, in that chaos, I felt strangely calm; I didn't feel discomfort; I only felt relief that my admission was done.

Perhaps, those journeys where I was squeezed between strangers with no space to stretch have taught me endurance and acceptance in a way comfort never could and carried me into a future I never dared to dream of.

By the time I got home, I was exhausted physically and emotionally. I was drained and fell sick soon after. I didn't know it then, but that train journey had quietly become one of the most important chapters of my life.

A few days later, I got an opportunity to switch my branch from Electrical to Mechanical. But the thought of making another trip to Mumbai, another long, gruelling ride, completely overwhelmed me. I just didn't have it in me. So, I stayed with Electrical.

And that's how the world got another Electrical Engineer, me. (And a good one, I'd like to think!)

Throughout college, I did my best and managed to get good grades. I made the most of what I had. I didn't have fancy or extra resources, but I never let that stop me.

Looking back, I realise that if I had better guidance, maybe I would have repeated the medical entrance. Maybe I'd have "Dr." before my name today. If I had better means, maybe I would have taken that second train ride and changed my branch. But those "maybes" don't weigh me down. They remind me of something important: I did what I could, with what I had, and I am proud of that.

It wasn't a smooth journey; there were missed opportunities, limited resources, and tough decisions made out of constraints rather than choice. But in all that "less," I unknowingly grew more.

More resilient. More grateful. More aware of the value of what I had.

That officer's kind gesture, that TTE's understanding, that humble roadside meal; none of these were grand events. But they gave me something no textbook or app ever could-*The Perspective.*

We live in a time where flights have replaced trains, apps replace people, and advice flows faster than thought. But nothing I have gained in life, not success, not position, not comfort, has ever taught me more than that one slow, hot, unpredictable train ride.

In that chaos, I learned resilience. In discomfort, I discovered humility. In moments of uncertainty, I found my strength.

> ***"I grew up with less. But I carry more within me because of it."***

Memory Note

Even though my plans changed and things were hard, I learned important lessons like patience, kindness, and staying strong. Small moments and challenges helped me grow more than I expected. This journey taught me that success is not just about titles but about how we handle life's ups and downs.

11
The Recommendation

The journey to college was only the beginning. The real concern was accommodation. Without a confirmed college hostel accommodation in Mumbai, continuing my education would have been nearly impossible, as renting a room in Mumbai and studying was beyond our means. So, before stepping into classrooms, I had to secure a place to sleep.

I travelled to Mumbai with my father for the hostel admission process. My uncle had arranged a pass for me to stay for a night at the MLA Hostel building through the kind reference of the MLA representing our constituency. Like many times before and after, my uncle stood behind the scenes and made things easier for me. I will always remain grateful for his constant presence in my journey.

At the same time, one of my mother's colleagues had connected us to someone in Mumbai who could help us seek a recommendation from the Minister of State for Social Welfare.

In those days, I believed recommendation was necessary.

We visited the concerned person,he asked me a few simple questions like where I was from, what I had studied, and what I planned to pursue. He listened quietly and offered us to stay in his meditation centre for the night. *"Come tomorrow morning,"* he said. *"My assistant will give you a note."*

That night, lying on the simple bedding at the common hall, I kept thinking about how many people were involved in helping me secure something as basic as a hostel seat. My father said little, but I could sense his concern. For him, this was not just about accommodation. It was about whether his son would be able to survive in a city as large and unfamiliar as Mumbai.

The next morning, we received the note and went to *Mantralaya,* the state secretariat. It was my first time entering such a place. At the entrance, a police officer asked my father what was in his pocket. My father replied calmly, *"Balm."* The officer looked surprised and repeated, *"Bomb?"* For a brief moment, there was confusion and panic, but then the officer smiled. It was probably his way of easing the tension and making us feel comfortable. Soon, the misunderstanding dissolved into laughter. Even in a tense environment, small human moments found their way.

Years later, when I returned as an officer, I walked through the same gates and entered the *Mantralaya* by simply showing my identity card. No questions. No hesitation. The procedure was routine, but for me, it felt deeply personal.

Inside, I handed over the note to the Minister's Personal Assistant and was asked to wait outside the cabin. We waited for hours in the lobby. People came and went. Files moved in and out. I kept wondering whether our turn would come.

Late in the evening, the PA stepped out and seemed surprised to see me still there. *"You are still here?"* he asked. *"Minister Saab has already signed your recommendation letter. Please collect it."*

That day, I also learned something quietly, ministers do not always enter through the same doors as the public waiting outside. Power often moves differently.

With the recommendation letter in hand, we returned to the MLA Hostel building for the night. I felt relieved. I believed the difficult part was over.

The next day, I submitted the letter to the hostel incharge at the college. He looked at it and said calmly, *"Every day I receive such recommendations, but the hostel allotment process is transparent. Recommendations are not required. Students coming from far-off places are given priority."*

For a moment, I did not know how to respond. After all the running around and waiting and letter, I realised the system followed its own fair rules.

Strangely, I felt reassured. We had done what we believed was necessary. The rest depended on merit and process.

That evening, as we left Mumbai after two intense days, I carried more than documents in my bag. I carried a better understanding of effort, systems, and the quiet support of many people who stepped forward when needed.

Much later, during my days as an officer, while serving in the divisional office on additional charge as a Technical Officer, I was entrusted with the responsibility of reviewing work estimates for Technical Sanctions (TS) related to government tenders. Among the list of buildings under our jurisdiction was the same MLA Hostel where I had once stayed as a student.

When I first saw its name in the file, I paused for a moment. The same building where I had walked in nervously with my father, carrying recommendation letters and uncertainty. The same corridors where I had stayed for a night, wondering if I would secure a hostel seat. Now, years later, I was reviewing its maintenance estimates and administrative matters in an official capacity.

Life had quietly changed my position, from someone seeking help to someone responsible for oversight. I did not announce this coincidence to anyone. But inside, it felt significant.

That day, I understood something clearly. In life, we often run from door to door asking for opportunities. But if we keep walking with patience and effort, one day we may find ourselves standing on the other side of those same doors.

> ***The building stayed the same. I did not.***

Memory Note

Looking back, I realise we often believe that big doors open only with big recommendations. But sometimes, honesty and process work more quietly than influence ever can. That trip also showed me how life changes our position over time. One day, we stand outside waiting, unsure and dependent. Years later, we may stand inside with responsibility in our hands.

12
The Joy of Sharing

During my engineering days, I was lucky to be surrounded by friends who believed in sharing, not out of sympathy or necessity, but out of sheer warmth.

We were all from modest backgrounds. None of us had endless money or fancy things, but somehow, that never felt like a limitation. If anything, it brought us closer.

We had learned early in life that the real value of something wasn't in how expensive it was, but in the thought behind it.

I still remember the day one of my friends got himself a new pair of sports shoes. They looked amazing, bright white and blue with fresh laces; the kind you could smell the moment they came out of the box. He wore them for a couple of days but then realised they didn't fit him quite right. One evening, as we were sitting in the hostel corridor chatting, he casually pushed the box toward me and said,

"Tu ghe na, mala tight hotay." (Take them, they're tight for me.)

I froze for a second, not sure how to respond. These were practically brand new, and I didn't want him to feel like I was taking advantage. It wasn't a grand gesture for him, just a friend passing something along. But for me, it was more than shoes. It was the ease with which he shared, without making me feel like I owed him anything.

In our little world, this was normal. Things flowed freely without anyone keeping a ledger in their head.

Another time, my roommate offered me one of his shirts when I had my first campus placement interview. I had clothes of my own, of course, but this shirt had a sharper look, just the thing to boost my confidence.

He smiled and said, *"Yeh Tu pehen le, suit karega tujhe."* (You wear it. It will suit you.)

I walked into that interview feeling like I already had half the job. Not because of the brand or the fit, but because of the gesture behind it. There's a special kind of confidence that comes from wearing something given in friendship.

Back then, I didn't own a mobile phone for quite some time. But that never stopped me from calling home. Whenever I felt the need, my friend would simply hand me his phone with a gentle, *"Bolun ghe ghari."* (Go ahead, call home.) Until my mother bought me my first phone, this was my only lifeline to my family, and I never had to ask twice.

That small, unspoken understanding was one of the most comforting parts of hostel life.

Food was another area where sharing became second nature. My meals during college were sponsored by a corporate house, which would give me monthly food tokens. Most months, I managed well enough to save one or two of those tokens. I would quietly slip them to friends who were struggling that month.

No announcements, no big gestures, just a quiet handover over chai or dinner. It wasn't charity, it was just how we looked after each other.

Our academics, too, were never a solo effort. All my friends used to take photocopies of my notes before exams. If one of us understood a topic well, we'd conduct a small teaching session for the rest. Those study nights were a mix of seriousness and silliness, and perhaps that balance is what made us all learn better.

Hostel life wasn't just about studying and eating; it had its own flavours, quite literally. Friends who were from nearby coastal towns would bring delicious fish and crabs whenever they returned from home. That's actually how I was introduced to seafood for the first time. For someone like me, who had never tasted it before, it was an entirely new world.

Once, my roommate brought *Gond ke Laddu* (Edible Gum Sweet Balls) from home, and I instantly loved them. He told his mother about it, and from the very next time onward, she would pack a few extra just for me as if I were a part of the family too. It was such a simple thing, but it made me feel deeply cared for.

We also had some funny little "perks" in our friend circle. My roommate's cousin was a Resident Doctor at an Eye Hospital. Now and then, just for fun, we'd drop by for "free" eye checkups. We didn't really need them, but it became our idea of entertainment on a slow afternoon.

What made these moments special was not the material value of what was shared, but the ease with which it was done. Nobody kept score. If one person had something, everyone had it. If one person was in trouble, everyone was involved in fixing it.

Looking back now, I realise that life today is very different. We can afford more, own more, and maybe, in some ways, we share less. Back then, sharing was never a planned act; it was instinctive.

We didn't have to think about whether we could spare something; we just did.

Those days taught me that the truest form of wealth is not in how much you can keep, but in how much you can give without hesitation.

Some of the richest friendships are built not on grand gestures, but on small acts of kindness done quietly, without expecting anything in return.

Even now, when I think about those hostel corridors, the late-night tea, the whispered phone calls home, the smell of fish curries from coastal towns, and the sweetness of *Gond ke Laddu* perfectly stacked in a steel box, I feel an ache of nostalgia.

Those were days when life was simpler, but hearts were bigger. And in that simplicity, we found a kind of happiness that money can't buy.

> ***"Growing up with less, we learned to share more and that made us truly rich."***

Memory Note

Hostel life taught me that generosity isn't about having plenty but having enough to share. The gifts that stay with us are rarely the ones wrapped in boxes; they are the unspoken offers, the extra seat at the table, the phone passed into your hand without a word. In giving without keeping count, we discovered friendships that felt like family, and a kind of wealth that has nothing to do with money.

13

The Economics of Simplicity

Back in college days, life was built on small decisions that felt ordinary at that time but shaped a philosophy that I carry even today. We didn't have much, but we never felt the lack. Instead, we mastered a quiet art of stretching every rupee, every coin, and every moment into something meaningful.

We used to go for tuition every alternate day, depending on our class schedule. After the sessions, we'd head back to our hostel. The tuition centre was near *Andheri* station, and our hostel was just a short distance away. There was a *BEST* bus that could take us back quickly for a fare of three rupees. But three rupees back then wasn't just a fare, it was a choice.

We could spend it on the bus or save it and spend it where it truly mattered, like a steaming glass of cutting *chai* from *tapari,* priced at two and a half rupees. So, almost without fail, we walked. It wasn't that we were forced to; we weren't struggling in the harshest sense, but it was about prioritising.

A short ride home didn't feel as valuable as a hot cup of tea shared with friends under the fading light of the day. That walk became a part of the ritual. We walked not because we had to, but because that simple choice gave us more. More stories, more laughter, and more moments that made hostel life memorable.

The route we took became familiar, almost sacred. On the way, we passed by *Navrang Cinema,* a single-screen theatre known for its unshakable loyalty to *Bhojpuri* movies. The posters outside were bold, loud, and often unintentionally hilarious. Titles that made no logical sense, with poses that defied gravity and sometimes good taste.

We used to stop and admire them like fine art, but our appreciation usually ended in laughter. I still remember some of those movie names; they were an entertainment of their own, and they became part of our customary comic relief.

One evening, our usual walk gifted us a bonus. As we neared the *Navrang Cinema,* we saw a small crowd gathered. Curious, we moved closer. It turned out to be a film shoot. And not just any shoot, we saw *Ajay Devgn* in action, filming a scene for the movie *Halla Bol*. It felt surreal. For a bunch of hostelites saving three rupees daily, stumbling upon a film shoot with a Bollywood star was a jackpot.

A memory gifted to us just because we chose to walk. Those were the perks of frugality; the unexpected joys that didn't come with a price tag.

Saturday evenings would bring a different kind of challenge for us, an economic one! Our hostel mess would remain closed on Saturdays, giving the staff their weekly break, which meant we had to venture out for food. After a few weeks of trial, error, and the occasional upset stomach, we found our saviour: *Sharmaji ka Dhaba.* It wasn't fancy, but it was reliable and, more importantly, affordable.

We'd walk there in groups, already debating whether to spend on that extra roti or save those few rupees for a post-dinner juice. But sometimes, our routine took a delicious detour. Just before reaching *Sharmaji's,* we'd pass by a Gurudwara. And on some lucky evenings, there'd be signs of a *langar* with massive pots on the floor, volunteers serving with quiet dedication, and the comforting aroma of warm, simple, community-cooked meals.

The moment we spotted that scene, our loyalty to *Sharmaji* would waver. Actually, let's be honest, it would vanish.

There were other saviours too. If there happened to be a session at *ISKCON* that evening, we'd happily turn spiritual because the prasad that followed was nothing short of divine, both in taste and cost-efficiency.

Looking back, it was all a part of the fun. It was a mix of budgeting, bonding, and a little bit of blessed luck.

Even our phone calls home carried this thread of thoughtful spending. In the pre-mobile era, during the first year of engineering, we relied on public coin-operated phone booths. But not all booths were equal. Some were miserable with the seconds however, others, like the legendary one near *Char Bangla Square,* gave you fifteen seconds more per one-rupee coin. We knew the difference. So, we walked the extra distance to that booth. Again, this wasn't about being stingy. It was about stretching what little we had and making it meaningful. We didn't count coins, we counted seconds, sips and smiles.

All these decisions were miniscule like saving a few rupees here, walking an extra kilometre there. But together, they created a mindset. A way of living where less never felt like a loss, and small joys felt like luxuries.

Today, everything has changed. We carry smartphones in our pockets, tap to pay, tap to ride, tap to eat. Life has become frictionless, and yet sometimes joy feels more distant. That quiet satisfaction of stretching a coin, or choosing effort over ease, has faded from daily life.

But the lessons remain.

What we learned through these small decisions wasn't just how to save money. We learned how to find value. Value in conversation. Value in community. Value in chai, in walks, in laughs over Bhojpuri movie posters, and in the comforting rhythm of doing more with less.

This way of living taught us to see what truly matters and how little it often costs.

Even now, when I pause before spending on something convenient, or when I choose to walk instead of drive, I hear that quiet voice from the past. The one that reminds me that *Growing with Less* has allowed me to *Living with More*. More awareness, more gratitude, more stories.

That's the economics of simplicity.

A life where the richest moments often come from the cheapest choices and where choosing less often means living more.

The economics of those days wasn't about managing expenses. It was about maximising moments and doing so with joy, not resentment.

> ***"When you grow up with less, you learn to spend on moments, not things."***

Memory Note

In those Engineering days, every rupee was a choice, a bus ride or a cup of chai, a dinner at Sharmaji's or the blessing of langar, an ordinary phone booth or one that gifted us extra seconds.

We learned that frugality wasn't about sacrifice; it was about trading convenience for richer stories, deeper friendships, and unexpected joys.

14
The Great Hostel Geyser Scam

In our engineering hostel, bathing in winter wasn't just part of the daily routine; it was a strategy game. A survival skill. A test of patience, luck, and sometimes loyalty. Picture this: thirty boys, one bathroom, and one electric geyser that worked for just two hours every morning, struggling to supply hot water for all. No backup, no second option, no hot water on demand, just that one little machine holding together the hygiene of an entire floor.

The geyser was switched on from 6 AM to 8 AM every winter morning. That was it. Two hours of hot water for thirty students who all had morning classes to catch. No one wanted to bathe in freezing water, but not everyone could get hot water either.

That's when the real fun and *jugaad* began-*The Operation Garam Pani.*

Some of us developed systems. Buckets were queued outside the bathroom at night like train reservations. The earlier your bucket was in line, the better your chance of getting hot water. You'd wake up and find a row of colourful plastic buckets quietly guarding their place, each one representing a student who wanted to sleep in for just a little longer. It was our unofficial hot water booking system.

But not everyone followed the rules.

Some got up at 5 AM, well before the geyser turned on, just to stand guard over their bucket. We called them "geyser guards." Brave warriors of warmth. They'd stand there half-asleep, towel on shoulder, hoodie pulled tight, keeping an eye on their bucket like it held treasure, which in winter, it actually did.

Of course, there were those who simply opted out. Bathing was not a daily event for everyone during those months. "*Kal pakka nahana hai*" (Tomorrow for sure I'll bathe) became a popular promise; always meant, rarely kept! Deodorant sales probably spiked, thanks to us.

But the real hostel legends were the *Paani Chors,* the hot water thieves.

They wouldn't line up their buckets. They wouldn't stand guard. They operated silently, in the gaps, slipping their buckets in between others or drawing small amounts of hot water from someone else's supply just enough to go unnoticed, but enough to enjoy a warm bath. It was precision theft. You had to be smooth, quick, and above all, shameless.

One of my friends became so famous for this that we gave him a title: *"Pani Chor Giroh ka Sardar"*-the don of the hot water thieves gang. No one ever saw him in line, but he bathed warm every day. When we gave him the title, he accepted it with pride, towel draped over his shoulder like a gangster's shawl, smirking like he'd conquered the system. And in a way, he had.

The geyser wasn't just a machine. It was the centre of a carefully balanced, chaotic ecosystem, a great equaliser that taught us the art of negotiation, the need for patience, and the ability to laugh at minor discomforts.

It wasn't just the geyser, though. The entire hostel was a masterclass in *jugaad* - the Indian art of making do.

Not all our hostel stories involved the geyser directly, but many were born in those early winter hours.

I still remember one morning when my friend, in a sleepy daze, grabbed a small two-rupee sachet of clothes washing powder to do his laundry. As he tried to tear it open with his teeth, the packet burst, and half the detergent went straight into his mouth. Now, instead of spitting it out (like any normal person), he calmly decided to use it as toothpaste. His logic was sound: *"Why waste it? Toothpaste hi samajh lo."* And right there, he began brushing his teeth with the washing powder! Later, that same friend went on to spend several years working in Dubai, leading projects and living in style. Whenever I think of it, I still smile. It was a small, ridiculous moment, but it captured so much of hostel life: funny, messy, full of little discomforts, but unforgettable and finding humour in the unexpected.

We never had big luxuries. No personal bathrooms. No 24x7 hot water. No one to do our laundry or clean up after us. But in those small daily struggles, something beautiful was built. A sense of camaraderie, creativity, and shared madness.

Our hostel authorities never tried to regulate geyser usage. Perhaps they knew better. Maybe they understood that this little chaos was part of our learning, an unofficial curriculum in patience, diplomacy, and resource-sharing. Or maybe they just didn't want to deal with thirty half-naked boys yelling about buckets before sunrise.

Today, I live a very different life. The water is hot whenever I want it. The geyser has buttons and timers too. No buckets. No lines. No *"Pani Chor Giroh"* waiting to strike.

But sometimes, in the comfort of that hot shower, I think of those winter mornings in the hostel, the shivering wait, the sound of slippers outside the bathroom, the laughter echoing through cold corridors, and the quiet joy of finally pouring a bucket of warm water over your head after 40 minutes of waiting.

Because those moments, however small, taught me something deeper.

They showed me that growing up with less wasn't a disadvantage; it was a blessing in disguise. We learned how to make do, how to adjust, how to find joy in little victories, and how to laugh even when things didn't go our way. A simple bucket of hot water became a symbol of teamwork, planning, and even rebellion.

In today's world, comfort is often individual. Everyone wants their own space, their own silence, their own perfect setup. But I am glad I had a chance to live in a world where things were shared not because we wanted to, but because we had to. And in that sharing, we found a connection.

We didn't just bathe together (not literally, of course), we grew up together.

So yes, the geyser was small. The queue was long. The water was never enough.

But the memories?

Overflowing.

> ***"The geyser gave us little warmth, but taught us big lessons in patience, sharing, and brotherhood."***

Memory Note

Those chilly hostel mornings, the crowded bathroom, the race for hot water, they weren't just about surviving winter. They were about learning life. In the chaos of buckets and borrowed warmth, we discovered patience, resourcefulness, and the kind of friendship that only forms when people struggle together. We didn't have much, but somehow, we always had enough. Looking back, it wasn't the geyser that kept us warm. It was the laughter and the learning we got.

15
When Festivals Meant Train Journeys

In those years of college in Mumbai, festivals didn't mean lights, sweets, or holidays. For me, they meant only one thing. Going home!

While others got excited about crackers or new clothes, I was counting the days to get on a train and leave the hostel behind for a few days. The real celebration wasn't Diwali or Holi. It was the journey itself from college to my hometown, from hostel food to home-cooked meals, from cold metal beds to warm conversations with family over dinner.

But as any student who has studied far from home knows, reaching home was a full adventure in itself.

Indian Railways, in those days, felt like an exam in itself. Booking a ticket with a student concession was like winning a small lottery. And the process started long before the journey.

First, we had to get a concession form from the college. That meant chasing down the college clerk, a person who had more power over our travel plans than anyone else. He operated on his own time.

You'd go to him, and nine times out of ten, he would say, *"Come tomorrow."* No matter what day it was, *"tomorrow"* was his favourite word.

So, we'd keep going back, form in hand, like schoolkids waiting for a prize. Once you got the holy signature, you guarded that form like treasure. Without it, the train ticket was too expensive for our limited student budgets.

Once the form was signed, we'd head to the railway station. This was before IRCTC (online portal for railway ticket booking) became mainstream or reliable, so the only way to get a seat was to stand in line at the counter and hope your train wasn't already full. It always felt like a gamble.

Sometimes we got lucky. Sometimes we didn't.

And if you missed the ticket? Well, that's when Plan B came into play. Some of us became experts at *"jugaad."*

I remember once travelling as a "companion" to a friend in the handicapped coach. I am not proud of it now, and it's something I'd never do today, but back then, it felt like the only way to make it home.

We didn't see it as breaking rules, we saw it as beating a system that didn't work for students with limited money and limited options.

Once, I had to book a return ticket, but the dates on my concession form didn't match. In a moment of desperation, I altered the dates by hand, thinking no one would notice. But the railway booking clerk saw it instantly.

He stared at the form, then at me, and said, *"Call your father. Let me explain this to him."*

My heart stopped.

Not because I was afraid of the fine, but because the idea of my father finding out scared me more than anything. So instead, I quickly called my cousin, asking him to help.

He came, spoke to the clerk, and somehow managed to calm things down. I still remember that moment clearly, as it was a mix of fear, guilt, and relief. That was the last time I ever tried anything like that.

But even after all the drama, once we were on the train, everything felt better.

The *Vidarbha Express* usually departed from platform number 18 at *CST*. That was a long walk, especially when you're carrying a heavy backpack filled with clothes. But the moment the train's whistle blew, the excitement began.

We would sit anywhere, often squeezing five people onto a three-person berth, talking, laughing, and sharing stories of hostel life and the things we missed about home. None of us had packed food; that was never part of the plan.

Because our real feast was at *Igatpuri* station.

No matter how crowded or sleepy we were, we would always get down there. That short stop was like a food festival, a hot plate of spicy *Aloopuri* and the smell of fresh snacks rising into the cool air. It was our tradition.

On one such journey, when we were enjoying our *Aloopuri* at *Igatpuri* station, we spotted someone familiar, our own professor, standing on the platform!

At first, we froze. Should we hide? Act serious?

But then, being the bold hostelites we were, we walked up to him and started a casual conversation. Somewhere in between, we said, *"Sir, the exam paper for the Microprocessor subject you're teaching us... It was really tough."* We were trying to casually convince him to be a bit lenient while checking our answer sheets.

He smiled, but gave nothing away. We don't know if it worked. But at least we tried over a plate of *Aloopuri*, of course.

The rest of the train journey was filled with classic Indian Railway experiences like chai vendors shouting, kids crying, fans that barely worked, and people asking, *"Thoda adjust kar lo"* (Please make space and adjust). But none of that bothered us. We were going home!

There were times when we didn't even have confirmed seats. We'd sit near the door or sleep under the berth. But it didn't matter. We had snacks, we had stories, and we had each other.

The closer we got to home, the more excited we became. We'd start planning what to eat first, which friend to meet, and how to spend the next few days at home before we had to come back again.

Those train rides were uncomfortable. They were messy, loud, and tiring. But they were also full of life.

We didn't have headphones or streaming apps. We had conversations. We didn't have privacy. We had people. We didn't travel fast. But we travelled with purpose.

Today, I can book a flight or a luxury train in seconds. I don't need a concession form, I don't wait in line, and I don't have to run to platform no 18. But strangely, I don't remember any of those recent journeys.

What I do remember are those crowded trains, the smell of *Aloopuri* at *Igatpuri,* the thrill of getting a seat near the window, and the joy of seeing my hometown station finally appear.

Those journeys weren't perfect. But those were ours.

Those were part of a time when we had little, but we made the most of it. When going home wasn't about speed, but about feeling. When every step, from chasing a clerk to begging for lenient checking at a station, added to the experience.

We grew up with less- less money, less comfort, fewer options. But in the process, we learned how to live with more- more gratitude, more humour, more friendship, and more stories.

And those train journeys during festivals?

They weren't just about reaching home.

They were about understanding what "home" really meant.

> ***"We travelled light on comfort, but heavy on memories."***

Memory Note

Those train journeys weren't just a means to get home but a reminder that even with limited money, no confirmed seats, and borrowed time, we created moments that stayed with us forever. The waiting, the mess, the laughter, the food at Igatpuri, they weren't inconveniences; they were the journey itself. We didn't grow up with comforts, but we grew up with connections and that made all the difference.

16

Cycle Wala Idli Anna – Feeding Minds and Stomach

Back in my first year of engineering, weekends meant long hours of tuition classes in *Hindu Colony, Dadar*. They were not just classes, they were marathons. The sessions would run for almost ten hours, morning and afternoon, combined with short tea breaks and a lunch break in between. Those breaks were not just pauses in the day; they were our lifelines.

And the hero of every break was a man we all called *Idlianna.*

He wasn't famous like a celebrity, but for us, he was a star. His setup was as humble as it was perfect. On the handlebar of his old bicycle hung two large steel containers, one filled with fresh coconut chutney, the other with hot sambar. On the back carrier sat big pots, covered with cloth, holding steaming *Idlis* and golden-brown *vadas*. Tied to the front bar was a small box containing fiery red *chutney*.

With this simple arrangement, *Idlianna* fed an entire batch of hungry students.

It didn't matter whether you were a first-bencher or a backbencher; when break time came, everyone's attention shifted to the gate, waiting for that familiar bicycle to arrive.

If you wanted an *Idli* with extra red chutney, you had to be quick. The race to be first in line for an *Idli* with extra red chutney was as intense as trying to catch a *Virar fast* train at peak hour. If some overenthusiastic student dared to ask a question just before the break, we would silently curse him because those few lost minutes could mean missing out on the red chutney altogether!

Looking back now, it's funny how little things meant so much to us.

A plate of hot *Idlis* was not just food, it was warmth, energy, and a small joy in the middle of a long, tiring day. We didn't have cafés or fancy canteens. Affordable and filling food had no alternative but *Idlianna's idlis.*

And frankly, we didn't feel we were missing anything.

At that time, I never thought about *Idlianna's* life. To me, *Idlianna* was just the man who served delicious food during breaks. But looking back after 20 years, I see it differently. I didn't know how far he rode every day, or how early he started steaming those *Idlis.* I only knew he would be there, without fail, during our breaks.

Now, I realize that while we were students chasing our dreams, he was working hard to feed his family, and unknowingly, he became part of our journey.

For us students, spending even ₹10 on a plate of *Idlis* was a small calculation. Many of us came from modest backgrounds. Every rupee counted. Eating outside was a treat, not an everyday habit. So, when we found food that was both affordable and delicious, we appreciated it more.

We didn't complain about the limited menu; there was only *Idli,* vada, and chutney

That's the thing about growing up with less: you notice the people who make a difference, even in small ways. You remember them years later, because their contribution was real, even if it wasn't grand.

Today, life is different. I can walk into any restaurant without checking my wallet, order whatever I feel like, and not think twice about the bill. My daughter has never had to wait in line for food from a bicycle. She doesn't know the thrill of being first to get the extra red chutney. But I sometimes wonder, will she ever know the joy of eating something simple, not because it's "the best in the city," but because it's all you had and it hit the spot perfectly?

When I think about *Idlianna* on his bicycle, I realise how those humble moments shaped me. They taught me that joy doesn't always come from abundance. Sometimes, it's about getting just enough at just the right time and appreciating it fully.

And maybe that's what Living with More really means: not just having plenty, but remembering the value of the little things that once meant the world.

> ***"It wasn't just Idlis we got from him, it was comfort, energy, and a piece of our youth."***

Memory Note

Back then, joy often came on two wheels. A humble bicycle carrying steaming Idlis, hot vadas, and chutneys that felt like home. Idlianna didn't just serve food; he served warmth, comfort, and a much-needed break in our long study days. His arrival was as eagerly awaited as the lunch break, and every plate carried the taste of simplicity. Even today, the memory of that bicycle reminds me how small things can bring lasting happiness.

Section - III

Career Beginnings

Stepping into the professional world armed with dreams, determination and lessons from simpler times, opening the door to living with more.

17

How Harsha Bhogle Helped Me Get My First Job

While studying engineering, I was what you'd call a sincere student, always among the top ten in the class, never failed any subject, and generally someone teachers trusted. On paper, I looked like a good candidate for any job. But deep inside, I carried a strange fear, a kind of quiet inferiority complex that made me doubt whether I was ready for the real world.

It wasn't about my academic performance; that part was fine. It was everything else. My communication, my exposure and my confidence when speaking in a group. I always felt like I was one step behind. Where others walked into campus placement sessions with confidence and clean resumes full of bold words and impressive hobbies, I felt unsure and underprepared.

Placements began in the last semester of our third year. The first company to visit campus was an EPC designing firm; well-known, well-respected, and well out of my reach. I couldn't even clear the aptitude test. That failure hit hard.

Until then, I had believed that studying sincerely would be enough. But that day, I realized something important : that academic scores weren't everything. That rejection wasn't just disappointing. It was a wake-up call.

I went back to the hostel that evening, not just upset, but deeply unsettled. It wasn't about missing that one company; it was about not being ready for what came next.

So, I started preparing seriously. We didn't have online courses or fancy career coaches. No YouTube playlists with titles like "Top 10 GD tips" or "How to crack interviews." No high-speed WiFi or AI mock tests. Just a few *B. L. Theraja, C.L. Wadhawa* and *P.S. Bhimbhra* type of reference books, borrowed material from seniors, and good old group practice with friends.

Around that time, I heard a story that both terrified and amused me, but in a funny, unexpected way.

There was this legendary company very hard to get into, considered a dream job by many students. During one placement season, their panel noticed a student had written "Rubik's Cube solving" under the hobbies section of his resume.

They asked him, *"Can you demonstrate it?"*

The student calmly said, *"Sure, but my cube is in the hostel."*

They told him to go get it.

He ran. Came back. Solved the cube right in front of them.

He got the job.

When I heard that, my mind froze.

I didn't even know that colourful square block was called a Rubik's Cube, let alone how to solve it. I looked at my own resume and thought, *"Yaar, what skills do I even have? Getting into the queue first and managing to score idlis with extra red chutney surely doesn't count as a professional achievement, right?"*

But somehow, the name of that legendary company with the mysterious green dot at the end of its logo, the one people often struggle to spell correctly, stayed in my subconscious mind forever.

I realised that campus placements weren't just about knowledge. They were about standing out. And I didn't feel like I had anything unique to offer. It was a strange time, filled with uncertainty, self-doubt, and some oddly timed humour.

However, the second company visited our campus. It was a JV of PSU (Public Sector Unit) in the oil and gas sector, and there I saw a different kind of opportunity.

The eligibility was very strict. Only a handful of us could apply. That meant fewer people, less competition, and better chances. My kind of company.

This was my chance.

I decided to give it everything I had.

This company had a group discussion round. Something I'd never done in my life.

I remember standing outside the GD room, heart racing, palms sweaty. I had always been shy about public speaking. But I told myself, *"This is not a classroom. This is your future."*

I don't remember the GD topic now. It was something to do with current affairs or business trends. But what I do remember is that, in the middle of the discussion, I somehow managed to quote Harsha Bhogle, the famous cricket commentator and speaker.

Just a few days earlier, I had watched a short motivational clip of his on my friend's Nokia N72 phone. Today, I honestly don't remember exactly what Harsha Bhogle said in that video. It was something about talent, excellence, mindset, and believing in yourself. And somehow, during the discussion, when the moment felt right, I quoted him.

I don't know how I remembered it or how I made it fit in the discussion. But in that moment, I found the right words at the right time. The panel seemed impressed. I didn't fumble. I spoke clearly. And for the first time, I felt like I belonged in that room.

I cleared the GD!

I went into the interview round with a new sense of confidence, not arrogance, just a quiet belief that maybe I did belong here. The interview went well. I gave honest answers, stayed calm, and did my best. Later, after two days of waiting, I saw my name on the selected list. And just like that, I had my first job offer. All because of a random video on a small screen and a line from a man who had no idea I even existed.

Harsha Bhogle never knew it (of course), but that one video gave me the confidence I needed in that moment.

And I couldn't help but think, what if I hadn't watched that video? What if my friend hadn't downloaded it on his phone? What if I hadn't remembered those words at the right time? In that limited world of no broadband, no smartphones, and no unlimited data, just a few kilobytes of inspiration had quietly shaped my future.

To many, it may have seemed like just another placement. But to me, it was a turning point. I had cracked it not because I was the smartest or smoothest, but because I stayed prepared, stayed open, and spoke up when it mattered.

I joined that PSU as an Engineering Trainee. The role was technical, tough, and far from glamorous, but I was grateful. That job gave me my first taste of professional life. It gave me my first salary, my first ID card, and more importantly, my first proof that I could make it.

I wasn't the only one whose life changed during those campus placements. One of my closest friends, who got selected along with me in the same PSU, faced a heartbreak. Despite clearing every round, getting an offer letter, and eagerly waiting for a year to join the organisation, he was denied entry at the very last stage because of a medical condition called colour blindness, which has no cure in the world. For a while, it felt unfair and almost cruel. But what amazed me was his response. Instead of breaking down, he stayed strong, tried outside opportunities, and eventually joined a private company.

Not only did he rebuild his own career, but later, when another friend from our batch who had joined with me realised he wasn't happy in the PSU, this same friend helped him find his footing outside too. Today, he has gone even further; he is a motivational speaker inspiring others with the same resilience that carried him through those difficult days.

Watching his journey taught me something my own success couldn't that life doesn't always follow the script, but strength and attitude can write a new one.

Later in life, I went on to do my MBA from a prestigious college in India. And after that, as fate would have it, I joined that same legendary company, yes, the same one that had once made a student run back to the hostel to get a Rubik's Cube.

I had once feared that I'd never be "good enough" for companies like that. But here I was not only working there but also recruiting students for the company. I had become the kind of person I once thought I could never be.

And no, I never asked anyone to solve a Rubik's Cube in any interviews that I took. (Though I did smile when I saw it on a resume.)

Looking back, I realise how much we didn't have at the time. We didn't have access, exposure, or endless resources. We didn't have 24x7 internet or mentors-on-demand. We didn't know how to "build our personal brand" or "optimise our LinkedIn."

All we had were books, friends, dreams, and faith.

We were hungry. We tried harder. We supported each other. We prepared in groups, pushed each other to improve, and celebrated every success, no matter how small.

We didn't grow up with more; we grew up with less, and that's what made all the difference.

My first job wasn't just a job. It was a message from life: that sometimes, one quote, one moment of courage, or one small act of preparation can turn the tide.

And yes, to this day, whenever I watch Harsha Bhogle commentate on a cricket match, there's a quiet smile that comes to my face. He never knew me. But in a way, he gave me my first break.

> ***"I didn't solve a Rubik's Cube. I solved something bigger, a self-doubt."***

Memory Note

My first job offer wasn't just a placement offer. It was proof that what you have is often enough if you make the most of it. Confidence didn't come from fancy words or practice in front of a mirror. It came from remembering a few powerful lines at the right time, and trusting myself enough to speak them. That's what growing up with less teaches you: how to make magic with whatever you have got.

18

The First Salary: The Door to Living with More

By the time I finished engineering, I had already learned how to make the most of very little. Those bus rides, hostel walks, cutting chai moments, and even strangers' kindness had shaped my outlook. Now, it was time to step into the next chapter, earning my first salary.

I had been selected for my first job through campus placements. It felt like the golden ticket. The company hired me as a Maintenance Engineer, and soon I was stepping into the professional world, wearing a new shirt and new hopes.

Around that time, a Bollywood movie titled "*3 Idiots*" was creating waves. If you were a young engineer in those days, you couldn't escape it. Every other conversation seemed to quote Rancho's famous line:

"Success ke piche mat bhago. Excellence ke piche bhago, success jhak marke tumhare peeche aayega." (Don't run after success. Run after excellence, and success will follow you.)

I was also deeply influenced by that line. In fact, I think almost every fresh engineering graduate in my batch carried that as their guiding light. For me, it meant only one thing, that is to focus completely on my technical skills. Learn every nut, bolt, current, voltage and everything. Be the best engineer I could be.

Because of this mindset, I used to feel annoyed whenever my boss asked me to do something outside of "pure" technical work. He often encouraged me to understand the business processes and learn the company's ERP system. But I would see it as an unnecessary burden and a distraction from my "real" engineering work.

At that time, I couldn't see the bigger picture. I didn't realise that the world of engineering wasn't just about machines, but it was also about how those machines fitted into the business, the operations, and the larger system. I just wanted to be in the workshop and maintenance sites, with the tools and the equipment, not in front of a computer screen.

Life, however, has its own ways of teaching you lessons. Those very ERP and business process skills which I resisted in my first job would later become the foundation for my future career, especially when I moved into consulting after completing my MBA. But at that moment, fresh out of college, I was too focused on "excellence" in a narrow sense.

If you have been following my journey, you'll know that *Andheri* has played a surprisingly central role in my life. Many of my earlier hostel walks, cutting chai moments, and even the *Ajay Devgn* film shoot happened around *Andheri*.

So, it was almost poetic that my first salary moment also happened there!

I was working on maintenance at a CNG gas retail outlet near *Andheri* station. My phone buzzed. It was a simple SMS notification, "Salary is credited". Those two words made my heart race.

That was it. My first salary. My first earnings from my own hard work.

It wasn't a huge amount, but at that moment, it felt bigger than life. I wanted to mark the occasion with something I could touch and see for years. Without thinking too much, I rushed to a nearby watch showroom. I found a *Cizer* wristwatch, priced at ₹780.

I bought it on the spot.

It wasn't a luxury brand. It wasn't expensive by today's standards. But to me, that watch was pure gold. It was proof that I could stand on my own feet.

The next day, I went to work carrying a box of sweets. I offered them to my boss and colleagues. My boss took a piece, smiled, and said something I'll never forget:

"This is the start. Many salaries will come and go. But this one you will always remember."

I could see something in his eyes; there was a mix of happiness for me and a flash of his own early days. It felt like we shared a quiet bond in that moment, an understanding between two people at different stages of the same journey.

A month later, my second salary came in. This time, instead of buying something for myself, I brought home a set-top box. For the first time, we had cable TV in our house, something we never had while growing up because of my parents' strict "no cable" rule. I had mentioned this earlier, but bringing it home with my own money felt like quietly closing a small chapter from my childhood.

Looking back, I think that was the real start of my "Living with More" phase. For years, I had grown up making careful choices, stretching every rupee, and finding joy in small things. That mindset didn't disappear, but now I had the ability to bring in more comfort, more experiences, and more memories without losing the value I saw in simplicity.

I went on to do many things in my career after my job at the PSU. I cleared the Engineering Services exams and joined Government service. I pursued an MBA from an IIM, switched to consulting, travelled the world and took on bigger challenges. But I honestly don't remember the exact date of many of those later milestones.

What I do remember is the feeling of holding that first watch in my hand. I remember the box of sweets on my boss's desk. I remember watching cricket matches on TV channels on our new cable connection.

And I remember my boss's advice about looking at the bigger picture, an advice I didn't value at first, but which later became one of my strongest assets.

When I retrospect about the lessons that I learnt from my first pay, and connect the dots now, I see how this moment wasn't just about earning money. It was about transition, from surviving and making the most of less, to having the ability to give more, enjoy more, and experience more.

It also taught me that "Living with More" isn't about spending wildly or forgetting where you came from. It's about adding layers of richness to life, whether through gifts to your family, shared celebrations with colleagues, or simply a well-chosen wristwatch that makes you smile years later.

The skills I learned unwillingly in those early days by understanding business processes, using ERP, and seeing beyond the machine became the stepping stones for my consulting career. That bigger-picture thinking has allowed me to help businesses, lead projects, and solve problems far beyond the technical level.

From the boy who walked instead of taking the bus to save three rupees for chai...

From the student who warmed his hands by a stranger's fire at the bus stop...

From the hostelite who laughed at *Bhojpuri* movie posters outside *Navrang Cinema*......to the young professional standing in *Andheri*, holding his first wristwatch bought with his own salary-it's been a journey!

The early days taught me how to live with less. My first salary taught me how to live with more, not just in material terms, but in opportunities, in generosity, and in self - belief.

Even today, when I see that old *Cizer* watch (yes, I still have it), I am reminded of that moment. The watch doesn't just tell time, it tells a story.

A story of patience, learning, and transition.

A story of how the smallest beginnings can open the biggest doors.

That's how my Living with More journey began, not with a big house or a fancy car, but with a simple watch, a box of sweets, and the realisation that I could shape my own life while still carrying the lessons of living with less.

> ***"That first watch didn't just tell time it told a story."***

Memory Note

My first salary was not just money. It was confidence. It showed me that I could stand on my own, support my family, and slowly improve our lives. I learned that growing in life is not only about skills or titles, but also about understanding the bigger picture. That first watch reminded me that progress can be simple, honest, and meaningful. It marked the moment when I stopped only managing life and started shaping it.

Section - IV

Reflections and Life Lessons

Looking back at moments big and small, finding meaning, humour and gratitude in the journey so far.

19

Past Miles, Present Smiles!

Some streets never change. You can leave them for years, live an entirely different life, and when you return, they greet you with the same sights, sounds, and smells.

For me, *Kharetown* in *Nagpur* is one of those places.

As a student, I walked through it every day on my way to coaching classes, my head full of formulas and my heart full of hope. Years later, I returned, this time as a father, driving my newborn daughter to a hospital for her vaccination, and the past came rushing back with every turn.

Familiar places, old corners, narrow lanes, all of it brought back a flood of memories from years ago.

This place was very different to me years ago when I was a student. Back then, I was a young student preparing for entrance exams. I lived in *Ramdaspeth,* and my coaching classes were in *Gokulpeth.*

Every single day, I walked nearly five kilometres passing right through *Kharetown* to get to my classes and then back to the rented room, which was shared with four other friends.

Looking back, I don't know how I did it so regularly. The sun was always hot, especially in *Nagpur's* summers. The noise of the busy city filled the air with sounds of traffic, people talking, and street vendors calling out. But despite all this, I never thought about how hard it was.

I never really complained.

I didn't feel sorry for myself. I simply accepted that this was my path, and I had to walk it. I didn't have a vehicle, and bus fares added up. So walking was the only option. What I had in abundance, though, was hope, the hope that all of this effort would one day lead to a better future.

Now, here I was again driving through the same roads in an air-conditioned car, with my daughter quietly sleeping in the back seat. The comfort and calm inside the car were a sharp contrast to the noisy, chaotic streets outside.

That contrast reminded me of how far life had come.

As we drove deeper into *Kharetown,* I began recognising small things. The same old dairy stall still stood at the corner where I used to stop sometimes for a cup of chai. A grocery shop, a narrow alley, a big white Bangalow in the corner with tall Palm trees, all of it still there, unchanged.

For a few moments, it felt like time had folded. I wasn't a father driving to the hospital, but I was a student again, tired but determined, walking those roads under the hot sun with books in my bag and dreams in my heart.

It's funny how some places hold pieces of us. Even after years, a single street can bring back everything: the sights, the sounds, the struggles, the small victories.

That day, I didn't just remember, I felt it all.

The biggest thing I felt was gratitude.

I was grateful for those tough years. For every step I took with tired legs. For every drop of sweat that fell in silence. Those miles made me stronger. Those walks taught me discipline, patience, and resilience. I didn't learn those lessons in a classroom; they were learned on the road, on foot.

They also taught me that success doesn't come overnight. It comes through quiet efforts, repeated every day. It comes when no one is clapping for you, but you still keep going.

Back then, I didn't know what the future held. I just knew I had to try. And now, sitting in that car, watching my daughter rest peacefully, I realised that all that trying was worth it.

Because of those hard days, I can give comfort today. Because of that past, this present feels meaningful.

It's not about the money in your account or the brand of your clothes. It's about what life teaches you when you have little. And how you carry those lessons with you, even when you have more.

We all start from different places. Some people begin life with all the comforts. Others, like me, start with less. But real growth doesn't come from where you start. It comes from the journey and how you walk it, how you grow through it, and how you hold on to your values when life changes.

As I drove past *Kharetown* and entered the newer, faster parts of the city, a quiet thought crossed my mind.

One day, when my daughter is older, I will bring her back to this area. Not for a hospital visit, but to walk those same roads I once walked. I'll show her the turns and corners that shaped me. I'll tell her the stories not to make her feel guilty for having more, but to help her value it.

Because the past isn't something we should forget. It's something we should respect. It's a reminder of where we came from and what it took to get here.

Life looks very different now. I have more comfort, more peace, and more freedom. But I haven't forgotten where I came from. I haven't forgotten those long walks under the sun or the quiet dreams I carried alone. What I have today didn't come easily. It came step by step through struggle, effort, and silent strength.

And that's what I hope to pass on to my child. Not just a better life, but a deeper understanding of how that life was built.

Because in the end, it's not just about living with more. It's about remembering the less that shaped us and honouring it every day.

> ***"We grow through what we go through and one day, that journey becomes someone else's comfort."***

Memory Note

The roads were rough, the sun was hot, and the days were long. But I never saw myself as poor. I saw myself preparing for something better, something more. I didn't have comfort; however, I had purpose, and that was enough to keep me going.

20
The Shadow That Never Left

As I have shared before, I studied engineering at a very esteemed government college in Mumbai. It was one of the top colleges in Maharashtra, especially known for its high academic standards. On the same campus, just a few buildings away, was a famous MBA college. That institute had its own reputation, one that we respected deeply.

As engineering students, we often watched students from the MBA college walking across the campus. They looked sharp, well-dressed, confident, fluent in English. They seemed so smart and sure of themselves. We used to admire them from a distance and wonder, *"How are they so intelligent? So confident?"*

Back then, we carried a sense of inferiority, though we didn't talk about it openly. We just felt it.

In fact, many of us were so intimidated that we even avoided going near their mess or canteen. We thought we didn't belong there. It felt like we were "lesser," less polished, less confident, less prepared for the world.

At that time, those feelings made a deep impression on me. I didn't fully understand it then, but those moments created a kind of mental block, a belief that people like them were ahead of us in life, and that we were always trying to catch up.

Years passed. Life moved on.

Somewhere along the way, that memory stayed with me. Maybe that's why I eventually decided to pursue an MBA myself. I tried, and by the grace of God, I got into a business school that was even more reputed than the one I had once admired during my engineering days. It felt like a personal victory.

I completed my MBA, grew in my career, and reached a point where I was recruiting fresh talent. Ironically, I ended up interviewing and hiring candidates from that same MBA college we had once looked up to so much. Life had truly come full circle.

However, life has a funny way of bringing old emotions back when you least expect it.

Years later, our Engineering college invited us for a reunion function. It was a big moment, catching up with old friends and revisiting a place that shaped our early years, felt nostalgic. One of my friends came along with her husband, and after the college-hosted dinner, we decided to take a stroll through the campus. Just to relive some old memories.

As we walked past the familiar buildings, the library, the old classrooms, the canteen, I felt a wave of nostalgia. The campus had changed a bit, but the energy was still the same.

And then, as we walked near the MBA college, I saw a group of current students laughing, chatting with friends, confidently walking around with laptops in hand. They looked exactly like how I remembered them all those years ago.

And in that moment, something strange happened.

That same old feeling came back. The same feeling I used to get back in college. A strange mix of admiration, intimidation and distance. It was as if I was still that engineering student from many years ago- a nervous, unsure, and quietly feeling "less than."

That feeling made no sense at that point in time.

I had come so far since then. I had done my MBA from a better institute. I had built a successful career. I had recruited students from that very same college. So why was I still feeling this way?

It made me stop and reflect. And then I realised something very important.

That feeling had nothing to do with "them." It was not about the students walking on campus that day. It was about "me." Or rather, the version of me from the past.

That younger version of me, who once believed he wasn't good enough.

Who once thought other people were smarter, more capable, more deserving. That version of me had created a belief, a kind of mental shadow, and that shadow had never fully left.

That old belief hadn't fully left me. It was hiding deep inside, waiting to come out when I was back in the same environment where it had first formed. It didn't matter how many degrees or promotions I had. Some emotional impressions from our younger days sometimes stay etched deeply within us.

That moment on campus reminded me that emotional memories from our early life stay with us much longer than we expect. They may fade, but they don't always go away completely.

And that's okay.

We grow older. We gain knowledge, skills, and achievements. But our emotions don't always follow the same timeline. Some feelings stay longer. Some shadows don't leave easily.

I had grown up with less, not just in terms of money or resources, but in confidence, exposure, and belief in myself. But now, years later, I live with more. Not just more success or recognition, but more awareness. More empathy. More peace with who I am.

Today, I don't feel inferior. I know my worth. I have worked hard, grown wiser, and found my place in the world.

But I still carry that old feeling sometimes; not as a burden, but as a gentle reminder.

A reminder not to let appearances decide my worth.

A reminder to honour how far I have come.

And most importantly, a reminder to be kind to the younger me.

Because that boy, the unsure and self-doubting version of me, deserves kindness. He didn't give up. He kept showing up. He tried, even when it felt like others were ahead of him. And if he hadn't kept going, I wouldn't be here today.

Now, when I think about those MBA students I saw at the reunion, I don't feel envy or distance anymore. I feel something else-"Understanding."

I understand that their confidence is not the full story. I understand that people often look fine on the outside while carrying their own fears and insecurities inside. And I understand that growing up with less taught me lessons I carry even now.

I might have lived with less confidence, but today I live with more gratitude for the journey.

Because true growth is not just about moving forward. It's also about looking back with compassion and honouring the path you have walked.

To the younger me, I say:

"You were always enough. You just didn't know it yet."

And to the person I am today, I say:

"Don't forget where you came from. Your strength lies not just in what you have achieved, but in how far you have come from doubt to belief, from shadow to light."

Today, I still carry that shadow. But it doesn't weigh me down anymore. It walks beside me, quietly reminding me of the boy I used to be and the man I have become.

> ***"Some shadows don't disappear, they walk with us, reminding us how far We have come."***

Memory Note

This experience taught me that confidence does not grow in a straight line. Sometimes it moves forward, and at other times old feelings return without warning. I have learned that this does not mean I am moving backwards or losing my way. It simply means that some emotions take longer to settle. Today, I do not fight these moments or judge myself for them. I pause, remind myself of how far I have come, and continue ahead with greater awareness and patience.

21
We Were All in the Same Boat

When I look back at my childhood and early days of youth, I realise it wasn't just me who grew up with less. In fact, almost everyone around me was sailing in the same boat. We all had similar means, similar opportunities, and similar limitations, but somehow, we managed just fine. More than fine, actually, we made the most of what we had and enjoyed every bit of it.

If I had a limited set of clothes, so did they. If I had to think twice before spending, they had the same thought. We never felt deprived, because it was the norm back then. No one had "more" than the others in any obvious way, so there was no comparison.

What we did have was a shared spirit that we wanted to enjoy every single thing to the fullest.

And we did.

One of my favourite memories is of a school friend who would fast for a day before the school's Christmas feast, not out of any spiritual discipline, but simply so he could fully enjoy the feast and "recover" the value of every single rupee he had spent! We still laugh about it even today.

At that time, it wasn't about being miserly; it was about finding joy in small ways and making the best of what we had.

Another friend from the hostel faced a tough phase when he fell a year behind in college. As per the rules, he had to leave the hostel. Living outside meant more expenses, which he could not easily manage. But he didn't give up. He started giving home tuitions to kids and even worked with a waterproofing company to cover his expenses.

Watching him juggle work and studies was inspiring, though at the time, we saw it as just life moving on.

I still remember one of my close friends, who came from a humble background and never once spoke about what he wished he could have or what he felt he was missing out on all through college. He quietly managed with whatever he had, never letting his emotions show. But the day he started earning, he went straight out and bought himself a brand-new *Hero Karizma* bike worth nearly 1.5 lakh rupees at that time. It was his way of fulfilling a long-suppressed dream, a symbol of everything he had held back for years. That bike wasn't just a ride; it was the voice of all his silent wishes, finally set free with his first paycheck.

Then there's the crash course story during my brief stay in *Nagpur*. We five friends were staying together in a rented room while preparing for our entrance exams. In the last few days of the classes, our monthly mess pass ran out. We didn't want to spend more for just a few days, so we found our own solution.

We gate-crashed a nearby marriage hall for food.

It was part adventure, part necessity, and a lot of fun. At the time, it didn't feel like a struggle at all, but just another story in our everyday life.

Looking back now, these moments could be called struggles. But for us, they were simply how life was. It was common for our generation. Everyone faced similar limitations, and everyone found creative ways to make life full of small joys. We laughed a lot, we shared without asking, and we stood by each other in quiet ways.

Whenever I see my old friends, we still share those same stories. The fasting before the Christmas feast. The wedding hall food adventures. The hostel's adversities. The part-time jobs. These are not just stories of "having less", these are lessons in finding joy, dignity, and friendship in what we had.

And somewhere in between, they taught us how to truly value more.

And as I think about it now, those early days were not just about surviving with limited means, but those days were quietly shaping how I see life today. They planted the roots for what I now call ***Living with More.***

But to explain what that really means, I'll have to take you a little further in my journey.

> ***"We all had our limitations, but they never limited our spirit."***

Memory Note

What stays with me from those days is not the lack of money or comforts, but how normal it all felt. Because everyone around us lived the same way. We were busy living life, not counting what we lacked. Those days taught me how to adjust, how to share, and how to stay positive even when things are not easy. Today, when life feels comfortable, those memories remind me to stay grounded and thankful. They shaped the way I think, the way I handle problems, and the way I value what I have.

22

Growing Up with Less, Living with More: What It Really Means?

Looking back, I see a life of limitations but somehow, it never felt limiting. We had little by today's standards, few clothes, strict rules, shared things, and missed luxuries.

A paintbrush lost meant missing a class. Cable TV wasn't allowed, so I heard stories about shows instead of watching them. I walked instead of taking buses, not just to save money but to enjoy a quiet cup of chai at the end of a long day.

And yet, even with these small struggles, there was joy.

A Sunday cold drink felt like a festival. A cousin's visit was a celebration. A one-minute call home became precious if I found the right coin booth. Scarcity made us value everything we had.

Now, I live with more.

There is no struggle to buy things. My daughter has every opportunity I once only observed, like painting, music, and dance. If she loses a brush, we replace it without a thought. I can sit in air-conditioned rooms, drive my own car, and stop for a cup of chai or anything without worrying about the cost. There's food in the fridge, clothes in the wardrobe, cushions on the couch, and cushions in the bank too.

But here's the strange part: when life became easier, some of the joy in small things became quieter.

Back then, a good mark in an exam or a kind smile from a stranger could brighten my whole week. Today, even big achievements can feel fleeting because we are already chasing the next one.

Growing up with less taught me gratitude and resilience.

Living with more gave me opportunities, but it also made me a risk-taker.

When you have faced scarcity, you learn that comfort is not the only goal.

I took the risk of leaving a secure PSU job to join Engineering Services and worked as a Government Officer. Years later, I took an even bigger risk of leaving that safe, stable government job to pursue my MBA. Those decisions shaped who I am today, opening doors I once couldn't even see. Without the lessons from my childhood, I might never have had the courage to take those leaps.

Both the lives, the one with less and the one with more, have shaped me in many ways.

Growing up with less gave me strength, perspective, and the ability to adapt. Living with more has given me reach, freedom, and the courage to chase bigger dreams.

What I carry forward now is a mix of both worlds, the mindset of less in the abundance of more. To pause and feel grateful even when the plate is overflowing. To give without keeping count. To enjoy what I have before running after what's next.

And most of all, I want my daughter to know not just what she has, but what it means to have.

Because *having* is not about possessions, it is about knowing their value.

I grew up with less. I live with more. And somewhere between the two, I found my real wealth not in the things I own, but in the courage to live life on my own terms, and the gratitude to smile through every season of it.

This is what ***Growing Up with Less, Living with More*** truly means for me.

It is not just my story; it is a reminder that abundance is not about how much you own, but how deeply you value what life gives you.

And this is where I choose to pause my story. Life has gone on beyond this through many roles and many more experiences, but I wanted to stop here, at the point where my roots and my growth connect. Because the purpose of this book was never to tell everything, but to share the journey of how *less* shaped me, and how *more* taught me.

If I had to sum it up in one line, it would be this:

> ***"The richest life is not the one with the most, but the one lived with the deepest gratitude!"***

The boy who grew up with less had already learned to live with more. The rest is only an extension of those lessons.

A Tribute

When I look back at my childhood, I realise that my journey was never mine alone. It was written with the sacrifices of my parents and my sister, who gave up more than I ever understood at that time.

We had a comfortable life in our hometown, a house of our own, familiar neighbours, and a setup my father had carefully built over the years. Yet, when it came to my education, my parents chose to leave it all behind. English-medium schools weren't available in our small town, and they didn't want me to be at a disadvantage. So, they packed up our lives and moved to the district town, just so I could study in a better school.

I never thought about what that decision meant for them back then. It meant starting again from scratch; renting a house, adjusting to a new rhythm of life, and letting go of the security they had built over the years. They never complained, never made me feel like a burden, and only reminded me that education was worth every struggle.

But perhaps the biggest sacrifice was made by my sister. She had to leave her own school, her teachers, her closest friends, and start again simply so her younger brother could have a chance our small town could not give. She adjusted quietly, never once making me feel guilty, though I know now how hard it must have been for her.

At that time, I was too young to notice these things. I was only excited about a new school, new books, and new opportunities. It is only now, as I reflect on those years, that I see the invisible price my family paid for my future.

Every exam I cleared, every success I achieved, and every milestone I crossed was possible only because of the sacrifices they made silently in the background.

My mother is no longer with us today. But whenever I think of that time, I see her face, calm and determined, making those choices without hesitation. She lived her life for us, and I often wonder if she knew how much her sacrifices would shape mine.

The life I live now is built not just on my efforts, but on the quiet giving-up of comforts by my parents and sister.

I often wonder if I can ever repay them. Perhaps not. But I carry their sacrifices in my heart every day. They remind me that nothing I have today was built by me alone. It was built on the foundation of their love, their selflessness, and their willingness to put my dreams above their own comfort.

For that, I am forever grateful.

Growing up, I may have felt we had less limited means, fewer choices, fewer comforts. But in reality, I had more than most. I had a family that was willing to give up their "more" so that I could have mine.

Carry It Forward

If these stories reminded you of your own journey, pause for a moment. Think about what "less" meant in your life and what "more" means to you today.

Your Memory Note